Make
The Book of
Revelation
Easy to Understand
By Using the
Old Testament
As Your Guide

A Jesus Centered Book
By Terrance Rhodes

This work is non-fiction.

Text and title copyright
© by Terrance G. Rhodes
All rights reserved.

Cover design by Jackie Aquino and Terrance Rhodes
Editor Diane Cowie

Amazon, Amazon Log
Published by Amazon are Trademarks of Amazon.com and its affiliates.

Published Independently
ISBN 9798332014642

*A special thanks to my brother Chris, for encouraging me to write this book.
*And for my beautiful wife, Jackie, who everyday inspires me to be more creative.
Thanks also to Pastor Bill Schott, for always making it about Jesus.

Visit Our Website: MessengerforJesus.com

All Scripture Quoted is from the New King James Version. Used by permission.

<u>Edited by Diane Cowie</u>

Table of Contents

INTRODUCTION

"Blessed is he who reads and those who hear the words of this prophecy, and keep those things which are written in it; for the time is near." Revelation 1:3

There is only one book of the Holy Bible that starts with a blessing. That promise above is unique to the Book of Revelation. Let's help you receive that blessing.

Cherry pick but don't stop! This book might be tough to read, so I want to encourage you right from the beginning, don't stop reading. In fact, treat it like a buffet bar and cherry pick! If you find a couple chapters difficult to understand, like chapters four and five, then jump back to the **Table of Contents** to find a topic you'd rather study. That's perfectly fine, as long as when you're finished with this book two things happen: 1) You know more about Jesus **because** 2) You better understand His Word.

I wrote this book to help make reading The Book of Revelation easy. Revelation can be understood. And the better we understand Revelation, the better we will understand the

Author of our faith, Jesus, because He *is a rewarder of the diligent* (Hebrews 11:6).

In the first four chapters, we'll give you three tools. Just three tools. My goal is not to tell you **what** to think, but to teach you **how to understand what you are looking at**.

Throughout the book, there will be questions at the end of each chapter. I also included a couple places for interaction. Hopefully, you'll have your Holy Bible next to you, **open so you can see for yourself the Scripture as we discuss it.** As you read through each chapter, test what you are reading. Test what I'm telling you.

Be diligent in prayer, asking Jesus for direction and understanding. And guard your heart with humility and love. Whatever you learn here, share with others… in grace. Don't allow your newly gained biblical knowledge to be something you beat others over the head with, but use this wisdom to bring your family and friends to the truth of Jesus Christ, like He would Himself.

Chapter 1: Would It Be A Private Interpretation?

*"the mystery of God would be finished, **as He declared to His servants the prophets.**"*
Revelation 10:7

Let's ask the big question to start this book: Would John's vision of the apocalypse be the only one we have? Would Jesus reveal something only to the Apostle John and to nobody else? Would we have to trust just one apostle's vision? I believe the answer is 'no'. But what good is my opinion without some great facts to support it or without some really cool connections in Scripture?

Here's the simple framework for this book: 1, 2, 3,... as in one gospel, two witnesses, and three tools. Plus we will examine all the key subjects of Revelation, like the scroll, the harlot, the beast, the mark of the beast and more while using the three tools. I do genuinely desire for all of us to learn together. From all the things I thought I knew before starting this project to where I am now, the truth is that none of us know it all. But I do believe with open conversations between brothers and sisters in Jesus Christ, His

Spirit will reveal more and more as we study His Word together in truth, unity and love.

One Gospel

The Gospel is redemption and restoration. I think most of us could add different theological addendums but ultimately we could agree to the gospel being the redemption of man by Jesus Christ into a restored relationship with our Creator. And the gospel is key to grasping the Book of Revelation. The Holy Bible starts with mankind in a paradise garden, in perfect relation with our creator God. So if our gospel, in Jesus, brings both redemption and restoration, then we should expect the end of the Bible to look like the beginning of the Bible. Right? We should expect the end of the story to match the beginning of the story. We start the Biblical story in perfect fellowship with God inside a paradise garden. Is this how we see the Book of Revelation end? Yes it is.

Two witnesses

What about the opening question? Would the Apostle John have the only vision of the end of days? There is a standard biblical principle to discuss. *"By the mouth of two or more witnesses a matter is established."* How can this add to our understanding of Revelation? If it was important enough for God to require more than one witness to establish earthly matters, would it hold true for heavenly matters? It was this question that caused me to begin researching this book. I was certain that the vision John had must have been confirmed by other witnesses. I encourage you, the reader, to study for yourself and to thoroughly test everything you read here. And have fun as you learn - just like I did.

Three Tools

Ok, so we've looked at one gospel and two witnesses. Now let's consider the three tools of research for the book of Revelation: **The Big Picture, The Language and The Chiasm.** *The Big Picture* is an overview of the gospel. And it's useful to keep things in perspective. As simple as that sounds, believe me, we need reminders of it as we tackle some complicated subjects.

The second tool, *The Language*, is probably the most useful tool because it's the easiest to use and sometimes the most fun. This is when we connect exact words or phrases from the New Testament to the Old Testament. I also think this tool can be the most exciting because it highlights the One True Author from beginning to end. There's no book like the Holy Bible because there's no God like Our God.

The last tool is sometimes the most confusing, initially, *The Chiasm*. Maybe you're like me and you grew up in a Christian home. Yet, for the first 40 years of my life, in Christendom, I never heard the word 'chiasm'. But once I learned about it, and took the time to understand this literary tool, it changed my biblical understanding forever. And I want that for everyone. We'll take two chapters to understand *The Chiasm*. However, no book on Revelation would be complete without at least one timeline, so this book has a timeline and it's called *The Chiasm*. But for now relax, we'll get there in a couple chapters and we'll have the graphs and examples to make it easier to understand.

Once we've got our tools in hand, we are going to tackle **The Key Subjects** of Revelation in chapters 11 -- 37. There, you'll find subjects like the mark of the beast, the battle of Armageddon, and the 144,000. So let's begin by looking at our first tool.

Chapter 2: The Big Picture

*"Declaring the end from the
beginning, And from ancient times
things that are not yet done, Saying,
'My counsel shall stand, And I will
do all My pleasure," Isaiah 46:10.*

One God, one gospel, one story – this is
The Big Picture of the Holy Bible. Years ago, I had
the pleasure of working with a ministry in Bercy,
Haiti. They had built a facility for a church on
their property and were looking to hire a local
Haitian pastor to lead the church. Because this
meant American money, they had a large
response from prospective candidates. The one
question given to the forty or so prospective
pastors seemed simple: what is the Gospel?
Believe it or not, there were 40 different answers
with only one – one pastor, actually giving the
gospel according to the Holy Bible. And he got the
job.
    The gospel can be given in a short or long
version, but there are some key elements that
every version should have. First, the Lord God
created everything, and made man in His Image.
The Creator then placed man in a perfect
paradise, gave him command of it, and gave him

a command not to eat of the tree of the Knowledge of Good and Evil. Man rebelled, sinned, and chose to disobey God. In grace, The Creator kicked man out of the garden, with a promise to redeem mankind and restore the relationship through a promised Messiah, the 'Seed' of the Woman. It has been by faith in this promise, that salvation is possible. And this promise was fulfilled in the perfect life, death, and resurrection of Jesus Christ. There is salvation in no other name. Jesus has returned to the right hand of the Father and will return again, to establish His Kingdom on earth, of which there will be no end to its increase. Amen. This is the gospel.

Today, we have the luxury of seeing the gospel fulfilled in Jesus. We have the benefit of looking back at the Old Testament prophecies through the lens of the life of Christ. But before the life of Jesus, the Old Testament was prophesy unfulfilled. And apparently, judging by how well Jesus was received and believed, those Old Testament prophecies were extremely hard to grasp and fully understand. Until the cross. Until His resurrection.

The gospel can be seen in the Old Testament book of Isaiah, who prophesied the crucifixion of our Lord Jesus, and did so very graphically. But it wasn't until we saw Jesus, lifted high, on the cross at Calvary, that the Old Testament language made sense. The future fulfillment of the prophecy gave clarity to the cryptic Old Testament language. But by actually seeing the stripes of the whip, the plucking of His beard, and the cross on which He was hung, only then did Isaiah 53 come into clarity. It was seeing the prophecy fulfilled that gave us understanding. As the saying goes, *hindsight is twenty-twenty.*

When you are driving, you look at the rearview mirror in front of you to see what's behind you. Perhaps the Book of Revelation might be like using a rearview mirror to look back into the Old Testament. We get a view in front of us revealing the fulfillment of all those Old Testament prophecies behind us. Do you understand that? We have a ton of future prophecies in the Old Testament which have not been fulfilled. And there are prophecies that will only be fulfilled in the last days. And it's really just the amazing kindness of Jesus to give us the future vision of Revelation so we could understand some of the past prophecies. We still might think the Book of Revelation is difficult to understand, but by far, Revelation puts a lot of the Old Testament prophecies into focus.

Consider *Revelation 19:10 "The Testimony of Jesus is the Spirit of Prophecy"*. He wants us to know the future, to trust in Him, to see His work finished, and He has included all of this in His Word. It's the very nature, 'the testimony' of Who He Is. There is no one like Jesus. Who else can 'know the end from the beginning'? And who else desires for us, His children, to know and trust Him to complete it? I believe He gave us the Book of Revelation as the key to see the Old Testament prophecies fulfilled and to give us hope. Sure, some of the Book of Revelation is still going to be difficult to understand, but it will be easier to do if we keep The Big Picture of the gospel in mind.

Chapter 3: The Language

*"Knowing this First, that **No Prophecy of Scripture is of Any Private Interpretation**, for Prophecy never came by the Will of Man, but Holy Men of God spoke as they were Moved By the Holy Spirit." 2 Peter 1:20-21*

Let's look at the second tool, *The Language.* The Book of Revelation uses a lot of Old Testament language. You're going to see exact words, phrases, numbers and quotes from the Old Testament. So, let's do something to make things easy. Let's eliminate as much confusing content from Revelation as possible. And let's do that by making sure we know the definition of **what the words actually mean**. We are going to use two rules.

Since we are calling *the Language* a tool, imagine holding a screw gun in your hand. As you flip it over, imagine seeing two warning labels on the tool. The first warning label says: 1) The rule of First Mention, and the second warning label says: 2) Scripture interprets Scripture. These two warning labels are two good rules that most scholars use for biblical study. Why? Because first, they help us understand the correct meaning of a word and secondly, they show us how the words are applied in context. We want to handle our tools with care and also see to it that we abide by these two warning labels. They are there for a reason.

The rule of First Mention is our first warning label. The first time we see the word 'love' in Scripture is not between a husband and wife, but between father and son. *"Take now your son, your only son Isaac, whom you **love**…and offer him as a sacrifice." Genesis 22:2.* The first mention of love can be linked to the gospel, the real emphasis of all Scripture. By understanding this first usage of the word love, we can properly understand how the word love should be used in all the following passages. And knowing the value God puts on love, we especially understand the love God has for us in that He sent His Son, Jesus, as His sacrifice for our redemption. If we ignore the warning label, and look for a different definition of love, we'll get a different understanding than the original Designer intended. That's how accidents and false doctrine happens.

Our second warning label says to let Scripture to interpret Scripture. I think some of the best examples of this would be by Jesus Himself. When Satan comes to tempt Jesus in the wilderness, Satan uses Scripture to tempt Jesus. How does Jesus reply? He corrects the **misuse** of Scripture with the **correct** use of Scripture. He uses Scripture to properly interpret Scripture. This warning label has been ignored by way to many people claiming to be experts. Avoid mishandling this tool. Guys! Use your phones. Do quick searches as you read through Revelation. Ask Google, or Siri, or Alexa for the first time a word appears in the Bible. Ask and see if there are other passages that make your passage clearer. Use your tools. Be aware of the warning labels. And have fun.

It seems obvious at this point, but let's reinforce it in print. **To understand the book of Revelation, you will have to study the Old Testament.** To eliminate as much confusion as possible, you need to know what the words mean and how they should be interpreted. Don't get stuck in the book of Revelation. Get used to bookmarking one passage there and flipping back to get the proper understanding of it.

Here's an example in *The Language*. In chapter two of Revelation, we have a promise from Jesus, *"to him who overcomes I will give to eat from the Tree of Life which is in the midst of the Paradise of God" (Rev 2:7)*. What *Language* do you see? This is the language of the Garden of

Eden in Genesis, right? And it's not accidental. It should cause us, the readers, to look back for understanding. This use of garden language should cause us to look back to Genesis and ask questions. Why? Because it takes us back to the beginning of the gospel story. The good news of the Bible is the promise from God to redeem and restore us back to His original will, which started in a garden. The Language is purposeful.

Don't be afraid if *The Language* is symbolic. Revelation chapters 12 through 18 are some of the most difficult and cryptic passages of the entire Holy Bible. They are incredibly hard to even read, let alone interpret. But readers, we have help. Look at the language of whatever passage you are studying and go find both rules: Where's the First Mention of your subject and what other Scriptures can help interpret your Scripture passage? Check and see if there are any other passages using the same words, phrases, ideas, or numbers.

If you're reading about a 'sign in heaven', take note that the first mention of those words are in the creation story in Genesis. *"And let them (lights in the firmament) be for signs and seasons." Genesis 1:14.* And then knowing the definition of 'a sign in heaven', begin your search for where to apply the second rule, using

Scripture to interpret Scripture. You might be amazed at all the connective passages to 'signs in the heavens'. Enjoy this study, and please, take a word of caution from me: don't jump to any quick conclusions. Be patient in your studies. Allow prayer, fasting, and gracious conversations with other believers to help shape and mold your thinking. And again, be gracious to others who are studying for themselves. Maybe they are not as advanced through their studies as you are. Fine. This is where we get to practice kindness, humility, love and encouragement to them as they continue. Don't allow pride to be a hindrance to your testimony or another believer's growth.

   The Language of the Prophets. The five major prophets of the Old Testament use language with direct connections to Revelation. I believe all of us should have a strong understanding of these Old Testament books. For example, Ezekiel 39 has a prophecy of the Feast of the Lord seen in Revelation 19, which follows the Battle of Armageddon. It is *The language*, and only the language of those two passages that connects them. If you weren't familiar with Ezekiel, it would be very easy to miss the connection. And by the way, the Ezekiel passage gives us more details than the Revelation passage. This is why it's important to make the connections in *The Language*.

But don't overlook the 12 minor prophets either. On my last count, I have about 30 connections from the small book of Joel to Revelation. So once again, take advantage of the Old Testament prophets.

What did we learn in this chapter? We learned *The Language* of Revelation is a tool which helps remind us to look back in the Old Testament. And we learned there are two warning labels to pay attention to, 1) First Mention and 2) Scripture interprets Scripture. If we properly use the tool of Language, and use this tool with its warning labels, we can eliminate a lot of confusing subjects from the book of Revelation by knowing the correct definitions and use of words.

Chapter 4: The Structure of Revelation

" The Sabbath was made for
man, not man for the Sabbath",
Mark 2:27.

What is a Chiasm? The word chiasm comes from the Greek letter "chi" meaning X. This is our structure of Revelation. I understand that for most of our readers, this might be your first time seeing this word. And I know it will take some time and examples to understand it. So this tool will be split into two chapters, chapters four and five. First, in this chapter, we'll look at the structure itself and then in the next chapter we will look at how it applies to Revelation.

Have you ever seen the ancient Mayan calendar? Or have you seen the ancient Aztec calendar? Or some ancient Indian calendars like the Vikram Samvat? They are nothing like our modern calendars. They are circular. It might seem odd to consider ancient societies had different calendars then we do today, but it's because they observed life and patterns in a different way than we do today. Most of us have been raised in western countries. We have been trained with western thinking and philosophy. The way we think today is evident in our tools for daily life. Our calendars today are linear: They move in a straight line from start to finish. But that wasn't alway the case.

Think of any modern day fairy tale story. The beginning starts low, like with a frog as the main character. Then we begin to go up in the story as the frog falls in love with the princess. We go further up as the princess kisses the frog and the frog turns into a prince. And then we're off to the moon as the prince and princess get married and live happily ever after! Up, up and away. The typical western style of writing starts low and finishes high. We've been trained to expect the ending of the story to be the highlight.

But it's not the way the Bible was written. True, the way the Bible finishes is fantastic, but it's not the emphasis of the text. The emphasis or main point is not always at the end. It's the emphasis, or the main point of the text, that we will call **The Apex** from here on out. The apex of the Bible is Jesus living, dying, and resurrecting. That's the emphasis of the Bible and it doesn't happen at the end. If the life, death, and resurrection of Jesus never happened, then the rest of the biblical story means nothing. It would be a book full of promises, unkept. But because Jesus did live the perfect life, and died a sacrificial death, which was overcome with the resurrection, then both the beginning and end of the Holy Bible have value. They have value because of Jesus. The apex of Scripture is Jesus.

Here's an Old Testament example of finding the apex of a story by looking at the text, not just the narrative. It's the story of Noah. We start with Noah being the last of his kind – righteous before the Lord. Then we see the Creator charge Noah with building an ark. The story builds up. We then see the family of our hero get on the ark, with the animals, and they go through the flood. And we see this phrase right in the middle of the story, in Genesis 8:1, "then God remembered Noah". Huh? What does that mean? But we continue on with the story. Noah's family survives the flood, they exit the ark, but then things kinda go down hill. Noah turns to wine and by chapter 19 we see the depravity of Sodom. It can feel like the great reset of the ark didn't do anything. So what are we looking at? And what's with that seemingly random phrase right there in the middle: "God remembered Noah"? As if an all-knowing God could possibly forget the last man on the Earth, right?

If it seems confusing, it's because it's part of a different writing style. It's not a western-cultured story. And it may seem a bit ridiculous to point this out, but it's a Hebrew Story, using a Hebrew writing style called *The Chiasm*.

So maybe it's time to ask, 'what is a *chiasm*'? Before we do, if you're seeing this word for the first time in your Christian walk, don't be alarmed! I grew up in church. I went through a strong Christian education, even earning my bachelor's degree at a Christian college, all without ever seeing or hearing of the chiasm. That's why we are going to take this slow. We will look at the chiasm structure in this chapter, and then apply it to the book of Revelation in chapter 5. I promise you, if you can take the time to learn the chiastic structure, it will forever change the way you see Scripture. It did for me.

But first, let's learn to see a story the way a Hebrew would have.

K) Noah and his sons (6:10)
J) All life on earth (6:13)
I)   Curse (6:13)
H)   The ark (6:14)
G)   All living creatures (6:17)
F)   Food (6:21)
E)   Animal's in man's hands (7:3)
D)   Entry into the ark (7:13-16)
C)   Waters increase (7:17-19)
B)   Mountains covered (7:20)
Apex)   God remembers Noah (8:1)
B)   Mountains visible (8:5)
C)   Waters Decrease (8:13-14)
D)   Exit the ark (8:15-19)
E)   Animals in mans' hands (9:2)
F)   Food (9:3)
G)   All living creatures (9:10)
H)   The ark (9:10)
I)   Blessing (9:13-16)
J) All life on earth (9:17)
K) Noah and his sons (9:19)

Take a moment to look through your Bible, and compare the chiasm to your text. Do you see the same words repeated at the beginning and end of the story? Do you see the mountains **covered** in Genesis 7:20 and the mountains **uncovered** in Genesis 8:5? Use a highlighter to identify matching words or numbers.

This is the chiasm, or the chiastic structure. It is not a coincidence. And no, this is not the only one in the Bible. If you want to search "chiasm in the Bible" you just might be amazed at how many chiasms there are. There are 37 obvious chiasms in Matthew alone.

Below is another example, this time from Genesis chapter 11, just a couple pages from Noah.

G) the whole world (11:1)
F)   had one language (11:1)
E)   Shinar, and settled there (11:2)
D)   "Come, make bricks"(11:3)
C)   "Come, let us build" (11:4)
B)   a city with a tower (11:4)
Apex)   But God came down" (11:5)
B)   a city with the tower (11:5)
C)   that men had built (11:5)
D)   "Come,confuse the language" (11:7)
E)   Babel, because there (11:9)
F)   The Lord confused the language (11:9)
G) all the earth (11:9)

This is where the rubber meets the road. The structure of the text is the key to understanding the emphasis of the Author. If we are reading the narrative of the tower of Babel, it's easy to focus on what men were building. In fact, finding the tower of Babel is the life's work of some archaeologists. However, it's not the emphasis of the text. In the story of the Tower of

Babel above, mankind is rebelling. Just as in the Garden of Eden, mankind was trying to be like God. But... and it's a big *but,* but the Lord God came down. Men wanted to go up into the heavens, but we saw the reverse, the Lord God came down. All of man's efforts – uniting, colluding, building, and planning end up meaning nothing against the judgment of the Lord God. The emphasis of the text, by seeing the apex of the chiasm, is on the Lord God coming down. The God of judgment, who is clearly Jesus (John 5:22), took the time to come down, look at man's efforts, judge man's intentions, and took action in favor of preserving mankind from itself. The emphasis of the text is meant to reveal something about the character, nature, and wisdom of Jesus. Jesus took action to preserve mankind. And if we need proof of His wisdom back then, simply look at today, at the the global community and its apparent march toward total destruction. Praise the wisdom of Our King, *"for He alone is wise"* Jude 25.

The chiastic structure is absolutely key to understanding the text because it gives two major gifts to the reader. First it clearly shows the emphasis at the apex, which is **the main point** to consider. And secondly, it allows the reader to see and interpret the text **with the text**. Let's talk about both.

First, the structure of the text clearly shows us the emphasis or the main point to consider. It's very easy to read a text or passage and get off point. That might be why there are so many different takes on one piece of Scripture. But if you look at the chiastic structure of the text, it is the very text itself – not a rabbi, pastor or priest – but the very text itself that shows us what's being emphasized. What a great gift to have in the text itself, to keep us on track. The Noah chiasm emphasizes the promise keeper we have in God. Despite the destruction of the world, despite the judgment and wrath poured out on sin, despite the 150 days of the flood waters and the time spent inside the ark, God is God of promises. He made a promise in the Garden to redeem and restore us. And He made a promise to Noah. Despite all the visible signs of destruction and ruin, our God kept His promise to Noah, and we can trust Him to keep His promises to us. The text emphasizes this about the character of our Creator.

Secondly, the structure of the chiasm also allows us to interpret anything unclear. Let me explain using the techniques of modern translators. The Wycliffe Bible Translators are world renown. They have translated the Holy Bible into some 1,786 languages (at last count). The Wycliffe translators are taught to use the chiastic structure when translating. Why? Because the text helps interpret itself. If you look at the two examples above, the upper portion of it chiasm mirrors or reflects the lower portion. Let's say we have a word in the upper portion that is very recognizable and very familiar. The upper portion then is easy to translate because it's also easier to interpret. However, in our example, let's say there is an unrecognizable or unfamiliar word being used in the lower portion. Well, if we know the chiasm, we can use the interpretation from the **recognizable** word to interpret the **unrecognizable** word. If you have a clear and easy interpretation of one portion of the chiasm, then by looking at the structure itself, you can allow the text to 'fill in the blanks' on the opposite side, knowing they reflect each other. Here's an example from the same passage, the Tower of Babel. This is a real life situation, where translators used the chiasm to help interpret a difficult word.

C) "Come, let us build" (11:4)
B)   a city with a tower (11:4)
Apex)   But God came down" (11:5)
B)   the city with the tower (11:5)
C) that men had ***unclear word*** (11:5)

If we were translating this text into a new language and had to figure out the ***unclear word*** in chapter 11:5, we could look at the chiasm for help. Yes, in the upper portion the text is *future* tense, "let us build". But in the lower portion it's *past* tense, "men <u>had</u>... ***unclear word***" The chiasm shows us the action in the upper section is mirrored below, so if the men *were building* a tower and then *finished* it, a reasonable interpretation of the ***unclear word*** would be the completion of the action above. They *were* building a tower, and the completion of it would be: they **"built"** a tower. The chiasm helps interpret the text.

What if we made an application of all three tools?
The Chiasm of *The Big Picture* using *the Language* of the Bible:

D) Man in holy fellowship with God
C)   The Garden of Eden
B)   The Exodus from Pharaoh
Apex)   Redemption through Jesus
B)   The Exodus from the Anitchrist
C)   The New Garden
D) Man in holy fellowship with God

- Big Question: Did you know the Holy Bible **opens with a wedding** in the garden? And do you remember Jesus opened His public ministry with a miracle, **at a wedding**. And did you know the book of Revelation **closes with a wedding**, the marriage of Christ to us, the church. Do you think that is a coincidence?

  *If you'd like to see another example of a chiasm being used for interpretation, skip forward to Chapter 27: 1260 Days.

Chapter 5: The Chiasm of Revelation

*"Then the seventh angel sounded: And there were loud voices in heaven, saying, **"The kingdoms of this world have become the kingdoms of our Lord and of His Christ**, and He shall reign forever and ever!" Revelation 11:15.*

Chapters

1-3	**The Church on Earth**
4-7	**True Kingship & Lordship**
7-9	**7 Trumpets**
10-11	**Testimony of Jesus**
11:15-19	**Jesus is King of Kings**
12-15	**Testimony of Satan**
16	**7 Bowls**
17-19	**False Kingship & Lordship**
20-21	**The Church in Eternity**

The structure of Revelation is a chiasm. And this is so very important to understand. If you're looking at Revelation with a western mindset, expecting the finale to be only at the end, you will miss the emphasis of the text. And you'll probably struggle with the interpretation of things you shouldn't have to struggle with. In fact, I'll say it here and now: If someone is teaching you the book of Revelation and has not brought up the chiastic structure of Revelation, you might need to ask 'why?'. That's how important getting this structure is. The structure of Revelation is absolutely key to understanding the book as a whole.

Let's find the apex of Revelation first by asking what is the main emphasis of the Book of Revelation? Is it the ending? Or maybe it's the battle of Armageddon? Or could the 2nd Coming of Jesus Christ be the biggest moment in the book? How would we be able to identify **the emphasis** of the Book of Revelation? Wouldn't it be nice if Scripture itself could tell us what the main emphasis is? This is where the chiasm comes in. The text **will** tell us what the emphasis of the Book of Revelation is.

There are 22 chapters in Revelation, and although the chapter divisions weren't added in until later, we can use them as a rough measurement. Let's fold the book in half. Twenty-two divided by two is eleven. So chapter eleven would be close to the middle.

Revelation 11:15 *"Then the*
seventh angel sounded*: And there were*
*loud voices in heaven, saying, "****The***
kingdoms of this world have become
the kingdoms of our Lord and of His
Christ*, and He shall reign forever and*
ever!"

Could this be the apex? Heaven
declares "**the kingdoms of this world have
become the kingdoms of The Lord and of
His Christ**". Does this seem like it could be
the emphasis of the book of Revelation?
After the rebellion of Satan and his angels,
as well as the fall of Adam, would this be
the crowning moment in all human history -
- when all the kingdoms of this world
become the kingdoms of God Almighty? I
believe we could say 'yes, this is the apex'.
This is the emphasis of the Book of
Revelation. We can verify this as *the Apex*
by looking at the surrounding text.

Chapters	
1-3	**The Church on Earth**
4-7	**True Kingship & Lordship**
7-9	**7 Trumpets**
10-11	**Testimony of Jesus**
11:15-19	**Jesus is King of Kings**
12-15	**Testimony of Satan**
16	**7 Bowls**
17-19	**False Kingship & Lordship**
20-21	**The Church in Eternity**

So let's start breaking down the graph. If you look at the first topic, you'll see "the church on earth". This <u>upper</u> section, "the church on earth" is in the first three chapters of Revelation, it's the seven letters to the churches. At the bottom of the chiasm, we see the "church in eternity". This is the <u>lower</u> section, which mirrors "the church on earth". At the end of Revelation we know we're united with Jesus, in the new garden setting. We don't see the word "church" in the last chapters, but we do see the "saints" in chapter 20. And we can make some connections. If we, the saints, are in glory with Jesus, then this is the church in eternity. Again, this is where the chiastic structure allows us to make solid, reliable interpretations. We see the church and Jesus at the beginning of Revelation, so we should look for the church being with Jesus at the end -- and that's exactly what we find.

The second topic is 'Kingship and Lordship'. In the upper section, this would be Revelations chapters 4-7. *The Big Picture* for these chapters is the true kingship, and the true ownership over all. And if you apply this to the lower section, chapters 17-20, you'll find kingship and lordship, but there it's the false kingship and lordship of Satan. Guys! This is huge. Chapters 17-20 in Revelation are massively metaphorical, cryptic, and difficult to understand. There are thousands of online sermons with wild speculations covering these chapters. To get the right interpretation, you have to read these chapters in context. What context? *The Chiasm.* If you know the upper section is about the kingship and lordship of Jesus, then it's easier to see the kingship and lordship of Satan in the lower section. Take a couple minutes here and scan through chapters 17-20 of Revelation, look for the elements of Satan's fight for earthly kingship and lordship. Look for the words 'kingdoms', 'peoples', 'authority', and 'judgment'. In chapters 17-20, the false kingship and lordship of earth is judged and Satan's authority is taken away. This is how to see Revelation.

The next topic following kingship and lordship is easy to identify. It is "The 7's". Below is a chart with the <u>upper</u> section of *Seven Trumpets* beside the <u>lower</u> section of *Seven Bowls*.

7 Trumpets		7 Bowls
1. Vegetation Struck (8:7)		1. Sores on Mankind (16:2)
2. Seas Struck (8:8)		2. Sea turns to Blood (16:3)
3. Water Struck (8:10)		3. Water turns to Blood (16:4)
4. Sun, Moon, Stars Struck (8:12)		4. Sun scorches Mankind (16:8)
5. Locust Army, pain (9:1)		5. Darkness, pain and sores (16:10)
6. Euphrates, 4 angels (9:13)		6. Euphrates, demonic miracles (16:12)
7. Great earthquake & hail (11:19)		7. Great earthquake & hail (16:18, 20)

The seven trumpets are the topic of the <u>upper</u> section while the seven bowls are the topic of the <u>lower</u> section. By the way, this will help us as we move through the book. These sevens will help give us a clear break from section to section. Here's two tips as you work through this topic. **First tip**: the timing of chapters 10 and 11 is unique. The 6th trumpet has passed. The 7th angel with the 7th trumpet is about to sound, but suddenly, there is a command to John to "*seal up*" whatever happens next. And we don't see the 7th angel again, with the 7th trumpet, until Revelation 11:15 which is our apex. However, if you remember to look at the chiasm, we still have a section in between. **The second tip**: the seven seals are not part of this section. It can be confusing because in the first half of Revelation we have both the seven seals *and* the seven trumpets. But the seven seals are included in the Kingship and Lordship. Maybe an easy way to remember to keep these sections separate is to remember a king uses his signet ring to seal what is his. So keep the sections separate, and only connect the seven trumpets to the seven bowls. Even after studying Revelation for as long as I have, I still use the chiasm to keep the sections separate in my mind... seven trumpets for seven bowls.

The last section before the apex is the 'Testimony of Jesus Christ' versus the 'Testimony of Satan'. The upper section is chapters 10 and 11. This section shows up abruptly. The 7th trumpet was about to sound when suddenly the story seems to take a detour. Two witnesses pop up in the story.

Who are these witnesses? I think we have an obvious reason they're not named. Do you remember when Moses and Elijah popped up in the story of Jesus? The disciples tried to worship them alongside Jesus. They wanted to build three tabernacles. But we worship God alone. Only Jesus was worthy of their attention. I believe we can connect that here. In the testimony of the witnesses, the messengers are not the focus. Their message is.

What is the message of these two witnesses? Well, what is the message, or good news, of all Scripture? It is the **FINISHED WORK OF JESUS CHRIST ON THE CROSS.** Because both the Old and New Testaments already bear witness to the finished work of Jesus Christ, then the book of Revelation doesn't need to include anything new here. The testimony of Jesus has already been revealed through Scripture. What were the last words of Jesus on the cross? "**It is finished**". I believe this is why chapters 10 and 11 are brief. We already have the rest of Scripture to know their message. The lower section which mirrors this, is the testimony of Satan. Chapters 12 - 15 are difficult to grasp. Let's keep these chapters in perspective to their counterparts. Chapters 12 – 15 compare the works of Satan to the finished work of Jesus Christ.

Let's connect some of these together:

- Both sections start with an angel descending from Heaven. The upper section's angel swears an oath to Jesus, " who lives for ever and ever". The lower section's angel is the fallen Lucifer.
- In the upper section, a book is given to John, symbolic of the Word of God. Scripture is the history of God's work for mankind's salvation. The lower section in chapter 12 seems to be a history of Satan's work against mankind, recorded through the eyes of Heaven.
- The two witnesses of the upper section are servants of God while the beasts in the lower sections are servants of Satan. Throughout history, the world systems have served Satan, which is why, during Christ's temptation in the wilderness, Satan offered Jesus the kingdoms of this world.

The chiastic structure is key to understanding the book of Revelation. Get familiar with the sections. Allow the sections to help you compare and interpret the opposite sections. Just like a hammer or screw gun, this tool will work better the more familiar you are with it. Go online, search for chiasms in other books of the Bible. And I'll challenge you here, to become so proficient with the chiasm that you can teach others how to use the chiasm to better understand all Scripture!

- Big Questions: Have you looked up 'chiasm' online yet? Have you found any chiasms in your favorite book of the Bible or in your favorite chapters? Does reading Revelation become easier with essentially dividing it into two halves?

Chapter 6: Two Witnesses

"Surely the Lord God does nothing unless He reveals His secret to His servants the prophets" Amos 3:7.

If you're ready for a break from those last two chapters and ready to start making some real connections to the Old Testament, here we go. Let's start by looking at one of the coolest relics of all time: The Ark of the Covenant. The Ark has been the subject of lore since its beginning. During World War II, Hitler wanted the Ark because he thought it held some kind of power. But he wasn't the first one to want the Ark. Two millennia ago, the Philistines actually got possession of the Ark only to find out they couldn't control it. They gave it back. And today there are countless stories and theories as to where in the world the Ark of the covenant might be. The Ark of the Covenant is fascinating.

Let's look at the construction of it. I really enjoyed the first time someone pointed out to me that even in the design of the Ark, we can see Jesus. The box was made of acacia wood (or shittim wood). Wood is often symbolic of mankind. The wood was then covered with gold. Gold and its purity is symbolic of God's holiness.

So the bottom of the box could symbolize mankind being covered by God. The top of the box, interestingly enough, had no wood. It was pure gold. The top of the box held the mercy seat, and therefore, being pure gold, it had nothing to do with mankind. The covering over mankind is only by God Himself. This picture points to Jesus. *"For there is one God and one Mediator between God and men, the Man Christ Jesus,"*. 1 Timothy 2:5

Then there were two witnesses. The Mercy seat, on top of the Ark, had two cherubim, one at each end. These two witnesses gave testimony to the blood of the lamb which was sprinkled once a year, by the high priest, during the Day of Atonement.

Inside the ark were three things: *"the golden pot that had the manna, Aaron's rod that budded, and the tablets of the covenant,"* Hebrews 9:4. These elements were themselves testimonies of different times when The Lord God made Himself known to His people. An Israelite child asking his father what was in the Ark would surely bring about some wonderful storytelling. Stories when The God of Israel performed great and mighty miracles in ways no one had ever heard of or ever seen before. These testimonies were to be passed on from generation to generation, so that the goodness, power, and provision of God would always be known to His people.

The Ark of the Covenant now seems lost to history. In its place, we have the Holy Bible. The Bible is packed full of different testimonies throughout history of when the Lord God worked wonderful miracles in the lives of His people. And just like the Ark did back then, when God's people open their bibles today, in their homes with their children present, what follows next should be wonderful stories and testimonies of when The Lord God has worked miracles in their home.

What is a testimony? A testimony is a substitution for an in-person experience. If you personally experience a bank robbery then you're the one with the testimony of the crime. If you were not there in person, then you would have to rely on the testimony of someone who was there in person. And it would be easier to believe the story if you had more than one witness, more than one testimony. Two testimonies, or two witnesses to a fact, are more believable than just one. Have you ever been asked to show two proofs of identification? Wouldn't one be enough? Maybe, but two makes it easier to believe. In a courtroom, two eye-witnesses help establish a fact. The ability to trust two or more witnesses in nothing new. The Old Testament gave a law to

God's people stating *"by the mouth of two or three witnesses the matter shall be established."* Deuteronomy 19:15.

We see Heaven also has a courtroom setting in the Book of Revelation, so it would be a logical conclusion 'that by the mouth of two or more witnesses a matter is established' in Heaven as well, if indeed, Heaven follows the same law God gave mankind. I don't think that's unreasonable to assume. The God of the Bible is consistent, being "the same today, tomorrow, and forever", so it would seem reasonable to hold Heaven by the same laws that He gave mankind.

Let's look at just the Resurrection Story:

- There were two witnesses, Mary and Martha, to exactly which tomb Jesus was buried in Matthew 27: 60-61.
- There are two or more Witnesses to the tomb being opened by an angel in Matthew 28:1-5.
- There are two angels as witnesses, one at the head and one at the foot of the place where they laid the body of Jesus, John 20:12.
- There are two or more witnesses to the empty tomb, found in Matthew 28, Mark 16, Luke 24, and John 20.
- There are over 500 witnesses to Jesus being alive after the resurrection, 1 Corinthians 15.

- And there are two witnesses to Jesus being alive in Heaven, Stephen in Acts 7:56 and Paul in Acts 9:4.

Jesus didn't leave it up to us to trust just one testimony on any of these points. He made sure we had multiple, believable, and reliable testimonies. Our God is kind and not willing that any should perish, especially from lack of believable testimonies. The more we read the Holy Bible, the greater the evidence is that Jesus has worked incredibly hard at making salvation possible to everyone. Often we think God is in Heaven just waiting to strike us with a lightning bolt if we do something wrong, yet **all** the testimonies of His Word reveal just the opposite. Jesus is actively knocking at the heart of every man, woman, and child, offering salvation through his precious blood.

It's no wonder why we see **two witnesses** in Revelation 11. Whether you read this metaphorically or literally, the emphasis is: **there are two witnesses**. It seems obvious to me that Jesus didn't make John the only witness to the last days. I believe John witnessed the same vision that the Old Testament prophets witnessed. When reading the Book of Revelation, keep in mind that no subject in Revelation is exclusive to John's vision. I'll say that again, **there is no subject in Revelation that you can't find first in the Old Testament**. There might be different details, but all the key subjects of Revelation are first mentioned in the Old Testament. If you take the tools from this book, *The Big Picture, The Language,* and *The Chiasm,* I believe you can connect both the testimony of the Old Testament prophets with the testimony of the Apostle John. I believe you have in the Word of God, the testimony of *'two or more witnesses'* for the Book of Revelation.

As for the two witnesses in Revelation 11, take your time as you explore the meaning of these two. Some claim the two witnesses might be Moses and Elijah from the Old Testament and they point to the Mount of Transfiguration as proof. Some claim they might be Elijah and Enoch because both of these men never died on earth and Hebrews 9:27 says *"it is appointed to men once to die, and after this the judgment."* Others claim this as a metaphor for the Old and New Testaments. However you believe, my friend, it doesn't change your eternity in Jesus. We might differ in our understandings, but thankfully, we are not saved by our understanding, we are saved by faith in Jesus Christ.

Chapter 7: Prophecy

"The Testimony of Jesus is the Spirit of Prophecy." Revelation 19:10

Prophecy, in the Oxford Language Dictionary, is defined by one word: Prediction. There have been countless prophecies, or predictions, throughout time. From famous historical figures like Nostradamus, or Rasputin, to the guy who's posting something right now online about the next election, there's no shortage of wannabe prophets who claim to have supernatural knowledge of the future. What would you guess is the number one type of prophecy? Maybe it's people prophesying about who the antichrist is going to be or people prophesying about the financial future? What do we think about when we think of biblical prophecies?

Let's look at *The Big Picture* of the Bible. From beginning to end, what are we seeing in the Bible when we look at prophecy? Think about the cosmic battle between God and Satan, good versus evil. We're studying a book which tells us the future outcome, right? That's what all these prophecies add up to. Individually they might seem all over the place, but as a whole, they are hundreds of little pieces of a puzzle which make clear a certain outcome. The finished picture of all biblical prophecy reveals a paradise scene with mankind redeemed, reunited with the Creator.

If you ask around, there's a general consensus that Satan is currently king of this world. The Holy Bible calls him the 'god of this world'. In what way? Perhaps as he holds sway to mankind's disobedience. Men often choose to bow to his will instead of bowing to the will of the Lord God. **But that's where biblical prophecy stands defiant.** Consider this: If Satan is really in charge as the king or 'god of this world', then why do all of God's future predictions, which just happen to be for key events, always happen just as God said? If Satan's goal is to prove God a liar, it would seem necessary to stop at least one prophecy, given in His Word. If Satan could stop just one prophecy from being fulfilled, then Satan would be able to prove God's not God, right? But yet everything we know about the prophecies fulfilled up to this point, says the exact opposite. The fulfilled prophecies are proof that God is in control of everything. Despite Satan's best efforts and despite mankind's rebellion, the Word of God stands no matter what. Whatever God says, happens. Think of the true majesty and power of our Great God and Savior! He can tell his enemies what He will accomplish, and there's nothing they can do about it.

There's nothing like the Word of God, unshakeable, unmatchable, deep and rich, and full of wisdom. What could be more valuable? That's a question for you and me. I Corinthians 1:18 says that *"to those who are lost and perishing, (the Holy Bible) is foolishness but to those of us being saved, it is the power of God"*.

I believe if you asked everyone if they would like to know the future they would say 'yes'. And if you had a source that accurately predicted the future, you would think that everyone would want access to your source. However, this is not the case. You see, the Holy Bible is batting 1000% as it predicts future events. There are differing numbers, but most can agree that Jesus fulfilled around 300 prophecies alone, by His life, death, and resurrection. Then, if you add up all the prophecies that Scripture records as being fulfilled, you get a ballpark estimate of 1,000 prophecies fulfilled on the low end and 2,000 on the high end. If that's not shocking to you I would offer two challenges: first, find the odds of a single prediction coming true. And then secondly, multiply it by either 1,000 or 2,000. After that, look for any other source that is predicting the future with the same level of accuracy.

The Bible gave the names of people, before the people were even born, like Cyrus in Isaiah 45. The Bible has accurately predicted battle victories, empires overthrown, astrological events, births, natural disasters, and so much more. The Holy Bible stands alone in this. There is no book on Earth that is anywhere close to the Bible in this one thing. Because of prophecy I call the Bible the only true **holy** book.

Here's the example of Cyrus that we mentioned above. Isaiah prophesied that a man named Cyrus would overthrow Babylon, and the Lord would shake loose the loins of his enemy, and shatter the bronze gates before him. (Isaiah 45:1-3) Then, 150 years later, history records it happened. The odds of this prophecy being fulfilled are close to the same odds of disassembling a Glock handgun with 34 parts, throwing the pieces into a bucket, and shaking them until they come back together in a working fashion. Reasonably you could say it would never happen, but mathematically it could happen, but the odds are so low, it wouldn't be worth betting on. That's just one prophecy.

Which brings us back to the value of God's Word. Possessing a book with knowledge of the future should be incredibly valuable. And we, as followers of Jesus, hold such a book in our hands. Unfortunately, the research studies out there say most christians don't even read it. Here's a book with proof of the supernatural. Here's a book that only God, who's outside of time, could possibly have given to us. And the vast majority of people never even read it.

Do you remember when Jesus instructed us to "do not cast your pearls before swine"? I believe He keeps His own commands. By giving us His Word, He has given us something priceless, something incredibly valuable. But He's also done it in a way that **only rewards the diligent**. "He's a rewarder of the diligent" (Hebrews 11:6). To a man who reads the Holy Bible but puts no time in meditation or in doing it, it's of no tangible value. But to a man who reads it, meditates on it, and does whatever he hears, the Holy Bible becomes transformational, life-giving, and of the greatest value.

> *James 1:22-24* *"**But be doers of the word, and not hearers only, deceiving yourselves**. For if anyone is a hearer of the word and not a doer, he is like a man observing his natural face in a mirror; for he observes himself, goes away, and*

immediately forgets what kind of
man he was."

The value of the Word of God doesn't stop with prophecy, because the real value of the Holy Bible is what it reveals about Jesus. The value of our Bible is what it reveals about our God, and our future with Him. We've been given something amazing. The Bible is a gift. Prophecy is a gift. We don't deserve it. There's no law or cosmic rule demanding that God has to give us His Word in written form, let alone that it has to contain prophecies. But yet, The Word of God has been given to us, and it's full of prophecies to give us hope and confirm the power of our God. These are gifts, extravagant gifts. And gifts reveal the heart of the giver. Think of the kindness, care, and thoughtfulness behind prophecy. Think of what kind of protective nature He must have, 'even as a hen covers her brood under her wings' (Luke 13:34). Consider 'his generous Spirit' (Psalms 51:12) with the abundance of prophecies. And give Him worship. He is all knowing and all powerful and by the fulfillment of prophecies He demonstrates power and authority from beginning to end. Amen.

The most frequent question that follows giving a gift is what? "What's the occasion" or "why?" Why would Jesus graciously give us His Word, and why would it be so filled with future predictions? The obvious answer to such an obvious question would be **preparation**. He, the husband of the church, desires us, His bride, **to be prepared**.

Think this through with me. Let's reason something about the nature of Jesus. Because Jesus is love, would love also demand hate? Would the love of Jesus also imply that He would hate those things which cause us harm? If we have a child that we love, wouldn't we also hate the things which would cause him harm. If a snake were to attack our child, out of love we would hate the snake, or at least hate the harm it could do to our child. We hear often that Jesus is love. (And believe me, the love chapter of 1 Corinthians 13 is one of my favorite chapters in the Bible. I often read it as substituting the word 'Jesus' for 'love' because Jesus is Love). However, with love comes necessary hate. For one to exist, the other is necessary. And it applies to more than just love. With justice comes necessary judgment, or how could we know right from wrong without judgment? With judgment comes a necessary law, without such there is no morality. Understanding both love and hate, justice and judgment, right and wrong are key factors in judgment day.

And there will be a judgment day for everyone, because eventually everyone dies. Did you know that? I was speaking to a group of young men one summer afternoon when I brought up death. I said '10 out of 10 people eventually die'. And I was kind of surprised with the young men's reaction. At first, they didn't believe me. They had to fact check me with their peers! They had to fact check that no one lives forever. Now if they thought that was shocking, how about explaining to them what follows death – judgment day.

I don't think we talk enough about judgment day. For us the saints, in Jesus, we know the judgment for us has been poured out on our Savior, Jesus, who offered His life a living sacrifice as a covering for our sin. But for the rest of humanity, those who reject Jesus as Lord, their judgment day is coming. But before that final Judgment day which follows death, there is a Judgment day here on Earth. Did you know that?

The Bible calls the judgment day on Earth, the Day of the Lord. It's a period of time when Jesus gives the inhabitants of Earth one last chance for salvation. The Day of the Lord is when we see all the trumpets and bowls of Revelation poured out on the Earth. **And it is during this time of Judgement when The Word of God will become the most valuable thing on this planet**. It will become more valuable than even scarce food or water. It will become more valuable than gold or diamonds. Because when judgment does come, and the end draws near, the only thing that will matter will be the decision a person makes on who they put their faith in. And for anyone who picks up a Holy Bible in those last days, and sees the events of their time prophesied, written in black and white, before it happens, will know the Word of God is undeniable proof of Who Jesus is. The Bible will be an undeniable testimony of Jesus Christ.

As for the church, the prophecies in the Holy Bible allow us to be prepared. John the Baptist, whose birth was prophesied, **prepared** the way before the first coming of Jesus Christ. John the Baptist's life fulfilled the prophecy of *"one crying out in the wilderness, make straight the way of the Lord", Isaiah 40:3-8*. The prophesied life of John the Baptist and its fulfillment were for one thing: preparation. Preparation of not just the physical, but of the spiritual conditions of man.

In fact, I can't think of one prophecy (maybe you can) where the hearer was not called into preparation physically or spiritually. Let's consider a few:

- Samson's birth was prophesied, calling his parents to prepare, and raise the child according to the Nazirite vows.
- King Jeroboam's hand withered and was restored at the word of the prophet, preparing the king to accept what was prophesied next.
- Jesus prophesied 'no stone will be left on another' preparing His disciples for the complete destruction of the Jewish way of life.
- Matthew 24 is to prepare the reader for the last days, in sequence.

"That the man of God may be a vessel for honor, sanctified, pure, ready for every good work" 2 Timothy 2:21.

Prophecy specifically, and the Word of God as a whole, are for the preparation of the hearer, as Jesus said *"blessed are those who hear the Word of God and keep it!" Luke 11:28.* This is where both the Word of God and prophecy need to hit home. They need to hit us right in the chest, and call us into preparation. We can look at the religious leaders back then and compare them to us today. Because what we know about the religious crowd during Christ's ministry isn't that they had a lack of Bible knowledge or a lack of prophetic knowledge. They knew the books of Moses by memory and they knew the prophecies by heart. So why didn't they see Jesus as the fulfillment of both? It's because they were spiritually dead. That's the short answer. Knowing the Word of God and knowing the prophecies was not enough.

They expected their knowledge of the Word of God and their knowledge of prophecy to fulfill **their will** on earth. They weren't concerned with God's will being done on earth as much as their own. This is why they couldn't accept Jesus. **Their will** was for Rome to be overthrown by a Jewish kingdom and for **them** to have leadership. The conflict was always over **whose will would be done**. They wanted an earthly kingdom according to their will and couldn't care less about a spiritual kingdom according to God's will.

According to biblical prophecy, there will indeed be an earthly Kingdom under Jesus Christ. And that kingdom will be led with spiritual guidelines, bowing to the will of King Jesus in all matters. Amen. This chapter is a call for us to prepare our hearts **to accept His will**, His future for us. We do not want to manipulate either His Word or the prophecies of His Word according to our wills or our desires. When we read and study prophecy, let's be very careful not to force our will or desires onto the text. Don't force your will on Scripture, but be willing to accept **the will** of God from Scripture.

Sometimes we get things twisted. The Christian life is not us inviting Jesus into our lives to help us achieve **our will**. We are not inviting Jesus into our lives for Him to follow us. Even in our society today, the man asks the woman's hand in marriage, and she accepts. He is the Groom and we are the bride. **We follow Him**, (Matthew 4:19, "Follow Me"). We are not inviting Jesus into our lives– to have Him help us build our kingdoms. It's the opposite. **We accept His invitation into His life**, and we help Jesus build His Kingdom. He's inviting us into His Future. And it is when we accept His offer, that He comes into our lives, and makes His home in our hearts.

Revelation 3:20 " Behold I stand at the door and knock. If anyone hears My voice and opens the door, I will come in to him, and dine with him, and him with me."

We don't lead our Husband, we follow Him. The christian life is accepting Jesus's invitation into **His will** and **His** plans **for our future**. We are His bride and He is our groom, and we submit to **His will** and His leadership -- knowing what an awesome, loving, generous, kind, and gracious husband He is. This is the marriage of the Church to the Lamb. So let's remind ourselves of this as we begin our study. We want **God's will** to be done on Earth as it is in Heaven, and not our will. Let the text guide you, don't you guide the text.

I want to close this chapter on faith. *"For by grace are we saved by faith, and that not of our own..."* Ephesians 2:8. Quick question: what's 'not of our own'? Look back at the verse. Both grace and faith are not of our own. The grace given to us is a gift. But so is the gift of faith, *'lest any man boast'*. But there is something to understand about the gift of faith. It can grow. Did you know you can grow your faith? Do you remember in Luke 17, the disciples asked Jesus to 'increase our faith'? Jesus answered with a parable which can be summed up like this, **'do what you're supposed to do and your faith will grow'**. Our faith, though a gift, can be developed and grown – just as all the gifts of God can be. We have so many prophecies already fulfilled. So at what point do we need faith? That's a legitimate question. The math behind just one prophecy being fulfilled is astronomical, but the math behind a thousand prophecies being fulfilled is absolutely mind boggling. At what point is faith a deciding factor? I would strongly argue at this point in human history, the probability of biblical prophecy being fulfilled is a near absolute.

Please, my friend, take advantage of your Holy Bible. Get to know the nature and character of Jesus Christ. His Word is a record of promises kept, of prophecies fulfilled, and of warnings to come. Exercise your faith by studying His Word daily as we are called to do. I am convinced that by studying prophecy, one can absolutely have 100% confidence in God's Word.

- Big Question: If mathematically, God's Word has been proven to be true, does that give you confidence in sharing Jesus with your community?

Chapter 8: Who Said it First?

"But in the days of the sounding of the seventh angel, when he is about to sound, the mystery of God would be finished, as He declared to His servants **the prophets.**" *Revelation 10:7.*

Who said it first? Take a look at the verse above. What does that mean to you? Or how about Amos 3:7 "Surely the Lord God does nothing unless He reveals his secret to His servants the prophets". 'By the mouth of two or more a matter is established', remember this from chapter six? And it would seem the end of the world as we know it, is a big matter. So let's start looking for other witnesses to the end of days. Let's look back into the Old Testament.

By having more than one witness to the apocalypse, God Himself would be keeping both the law and the traditions. Here is one of my favorite examples of Jesus keeping both the law and tradition: When Jesus performs His first public miracle at the wedding of Cana in Galilee (John 2), He is accused of not keeping the wedding traditions. He's not accused of not keeping the Law, but He's accused of not keeping the Traditions. However, I believe He was falsely accused here. Pastor Bill Schott did a teaching on this years ago and it has stayed with me since then. So the story goes something like this: Mary comes to Jesus, asking for help, because the wine has run out at the wedding. Jesus performs a miracle by turning water into wine. The wine is so good that the master of the wedding accuses Jesus of not keeping the tradition of serving the good wine first and the bad wine last. But that's because the master of the wedding never read Revelation 19. You see, Jesus served the best wine first. The miracle wine apparently blew everyone's minds and taste buds. But where's the bad wine? The bad wine is supposedly, by tradition, to be served last. Well, in Revelation 19 we see that bad wine being saved until last, until the very last.

"And He Himself will rule them with a rod of iron. **He Himself treads the winepress of the fierceness and wrath of Almighty God.** And He has on His robe and on His thigh a name written:

KING OF KINGS AND LORD OF LORDS.

And we all know we don't want a cup of that wine! Thank Jesus for His offering of salvation! Thank Jesus for the cup we do share, the cup of the blood of His fellowship!

- Big Question: Why do you think the Lord God chooses to reveal the future to us? In the Old Testament, often The Lord would send several prophets warning of destruction, before the destruction actually came. Why does Jesus use so many different prophets to repeat the same messages?

Chapter 9: The Heavenly Tabernacle

*Hebrew 8:5 "... **the copy and shadow of the heavenly things**, as Moses was divinely instructed when he was about to make the tabernacle. For He said, "See that you make all things according to the pattern shown to you on the mountain."*

In the opening chapter of Revelation, we see something really cool. The scene opens with Old Testament *language*. We see seven golden lampstands and a priestly figure, wearing a garment to the feet. From the language of the text, we understand we are in a sanctuary with a priest. But we have to ask the question, what sanctuary is this? This is not a sanctuary on earth, but this is that heavenly sanctuary from which the earthly tabernacle of the wilderness was copied. And the priest before us is none other than the High Priest, Jesus Christ. This places us, the readers, in the heavenly tabernacle, in the heavenly sanctuary of worship. Using your knowledge of the Old Testament, let's see **how many articles of the heavenly sanctuary are visible in the Book of Revelation**.

"I desire mercy, and not sacrifice" Hosea 6:5.

First, let's recognize the throne in Heaven as **the official mercy seat**. The mercy seat on the Ark of the Covenant was merely symbolic of the true mercy seat in Heaven. This is the throne of Heaven on which the righteous Judge of all the Earth sits.

> *"Immediately I was in the Spirit; and behold, a throne set in heaven, and One sat on the throne." Revelation 4:2*

What about the lampstand? We see one in Revelation chapter one, right? Do we see that in the Old Testament?

> *Exodus 25:31-32, "You shall also make **a lampstand of pure gold**; the lampstand shall be of hammered work. Its shaft, its branches, its bowls, its ornamental knobs, and flowers shall be of one piece. And six branches shall come out of its sides: three branches of the lampstand out of one side, and three*

branches of the lampstand out of the other side." (Three per side and one in the middle, seven lamps total).

What about the laver, or the water of cleansing, that we see in the Old Testament Tabernacle of the Wilderness? Later, in Solomon's temple it is called **the 'brazen sea'**. (2 Chronicles 4). Do we see this in Revelation?

*"Before the throne there was a **sea of glass**, like crystal." Revelation 4:6*

Next let's look for the altar.

*"When He opened the fifth seal, I saw under **the altar** the souls of those who had been slain for the word of God and for the testimony which they held." Revelation 6:9.*

How about the trumpets used for worship? Remember, Leviticus 23 has a festival specifically for these trumpets. (See chapter 18).

"And I saw the seven angels who stand before God, and to them

were given **seven trumpets**.*"
Revelation 8:2.

What about the golden censer with which the priest would wave the incense?

> *"Then another angel, having **a golden censer**, came and stood at the altar. He was given much **incense that** he should offer it with the prayers of all the saints upon the golden altar which was before the throne. And the smoke of the incense, with the prayers of the saints, ascended before God from the angel's hand. Then the angel took **the censer**, filled it with fire from the altar, and threw it to the earth.*"
> *Revelation 8:3-5.*

Next, do we see the bowls? If you're curious about the use of bowls in the Old Testament worship, look below at this excerpt from Exodus 25.

> *"**Three bowls** shall be made like almond blossoms on one branch, with an ornamental knob and a flower, and three bowls made like*

almond blossoms on the other
branch, with an ornamental knob
and a flower—and so for the six
branches that come out of the
lampstand. On the lampstand itself
four bowls *shall be made like*
almond blossoms, each with its
ornamental knob and flower."
Exodus 25:32-34. (seven bowls
total).

Compare to:

Revelation 16:1 "Then I heard a loud
voice from the temple saying to the seven
angels, "Go and pour out the **bowls** of the
wrath of God on the earth."

So yes, we see the bowls, and lastly, what
about the Ark itself?

"Then the temple of God was
opened in heaven, and **the ark of**
His covenant *was seen in His*
temple." Revelation 11:19.

Pay attention. Seeing Heaven
as a place of worship will make your
study of Revelation so much easier!

- Big Question: Does this surprise you? Does seeing all of these Old Testament articles of worship in Revelation surprise you? Pay attention. Seeing Heaven as a place of worship will make your study of Revelation so much easier!

Chapter 10: Jesus is God

*"I am coming quickly, and My
reward is with Me, to give to every
one according to his work.* **I am** *the
Alpha and the Omega, the Beginning
and the End,* **the First and the
Last**.*" Revelation 22:12 & 13.*

We know this book to be called Revelation,
but that's short for the full title: **The Revelation of
Jesus Christ**. If you're familiar with John's gospel,
the book of John, you might be familiar with his
view of Jesus. John knew Jesus to be God. Look
at his opening in John chapter 1.

*"In the beginning was the
Word, and the Word was with God,
and the Word was God". John 1:1.*

John believed Jesus to be God. In fact, look
closely at that last verse, and you might see
something more. Think about it, Matthew opens
his gospel with the genealogy of Jesus. Mark
doesn't include a genealogy because the
genealogy of a servant is unimportant. Luke
includes a genealogy of Jesus. But what about
John? Where is the genealogy of Jesus in the

gospel of John? Well, let's look closely at that opening verse.

"*In the beginning'*,-- that's where Jesus comes from,
'*was the Word'*-- that's the self existence of God,
'*And the Word was God*"--that's the nature of Jesus.

That's John's genealogy of Jesus, because Jesus is God. The last book of the Holy Bible is **The Revelation of Jesus Christ**, as God of Heaven, as God of the Scriptures, as King of all Kings, and Lord of all Lords. He is the Word incarnate. This is key for grasping the Oneness of God in Heaven. In Revelation the real 'Oneness' of God is personified in Jesus Himself. This point is hammered home by the language in chapter one.

Let's see this clearly. John hears the authority of God the Father in Revelation chapter one, verses 8,11, & 18,-- *"I am the Alpha and Omega, the Beginning and the End*...". This is repeated three times. This exact title **by God alone** can be found throughout the Old Testament. You don't even have to leave the book of Isaiah for this one point to be driven home. Open your Bible to Isaiah 44, get your highlighter ready, and let's mark these verses for future reference.

> "Thus says the Lord, the King of Israel, and his Redeemer, the Lord of hosts: **'I am the First and I am the Last; Besides Me there is no God**." Isaiah 44:6.

> "You are My witnesses. **Is there a God besides Me**? Indeed there is no other Rock; **I know not one.**" Isaiah 44:8.

> **"I am the Lord and there is no other; There is no God besides Me.**"Isaiah 45:5.

> "That there is none besides Me. **I am the Lord, and there is no other**;"
> Isaiah 45:6.

> 'Surely God is in you, and there is no other; **There is no other God.**' " Isaiah 45:14.

> For thus says the Lord, Who created the heavens, Who is God,

Who formed the earth and made it,
Who has established it, Who did not
create it in vain, Who formed it to be
inhabited: **I am the Lord, and**
there is no other." *Isaiah 45:18*

(Did you ever wonder where Paul got the authority to write in Colossians 1:16 that all things were created by Jesus? The verse above just might be that source.) Let's continue...

> **"And there is no other God**
> **besides Me, a just God and a**
> **Savior; There is none besides**
> **Me.**" *Isaiah 45:21.*

> **"Look to Me, and be**
> **saved, all you ends of the earth!**
> **For I am God, and there is no**
> **other.**" *Isaiah 45:22.*

Now if you look back into chapter one of Revelation, you'll notice we hear the same authority calling to John. Three times in chapter one, we hear the title **"I am the First and the Last"**, only to watch John turn towards the voice and see the 'Son of Man'. John heard the authority of God the Father and turned to see God the Son. John hears the 'God of Isaiah' and turns to see

Jesus. The obvious question is 'why'? And the obvious answer is two-fold: God is One (Deut 6:4) and Jesus is God. The Oneness of God is in *The Big Picture* of Redemption, which is now complete in Revelation.

As you read and study the Book of Revelation, you will be directly confronted with the Oneness of God– the Father and Son. It doesn't matter if you are unitarian, trinitarian, modalist, or anything else. In the book of Revelation, God is One.

It might be easier to see Jesus to think of it this way: Jesus is the true **Image Bearer** of the Father. Think of all the pictures you've seen of Jesus in your lifetime. Now, none of them are really what Jesus looked like, but we love to imagine what He might have looked like, right? I think that's a way to connect to the image of God the Father. The Holy Bible tells us in several different ways, that Jesus is **the Image** of the Father. If we struggle to picture, or imagine what God the Father looks like, the Bible tells us to look at Jesus – Jesus is the perfect **Image Bearer** of the Father. So if we want to see the Father, we look at the Son.

2 Corinthians 4:4 whose minds the god of this age has

blinded, who do not believe, lest the light of the gospel of the glory of **Christ, who is the image of God,** *should shine on them. 5 For we do not preach ourselves, but Christ Jesus the Lord, and ourselves your bondservants for Jesus' sake. 6 For it is the God who commanded light to shine out of darkness, who has shone in our hearts to give the light of the knowledge of* **the glory of God in the face of Jesus Christ.**

Jesus told the disciples,

"If you had known Me, you would have known My Father also; *and* **from now on you know Him and have seen Him."** *Philip said to Him, "Lord,* **show us the Father,** *and it is sufficient for us."Jesus said to him,* **"Have I been with you so long, and yet you have not known Me,** *Philip?* **He who has seen Me has seen the**

Father; so how can you
say, 'Show us the Father'?
John 14:7-9.

In Revelation chapter 5, you will see the
'*One*' on the throne handing the scroll to the
'*Lamb*'. The best way I can explain this is to
imagine a mirror. One one side of the mirror,
pictures Jesus, glorified on the throne. And then
in the reflection, pictures Jesus, as the '*Lamb
slain*', receiving the scroll. If the Bible itself says
Jesus is the perfect image bearer of the Father,
then none of us would be able to picture the
Father **better** than by picturing the Son.

> *"(God) has in these last days*
> *spoken to us **by His Son**, whom He*
> *has appointed heir of all things,*
> *through whom also He made the*
> *worlds; who being **the brightness***
> ***of His glory and the express***
> ***image of His person**, and*
> *upholding all things by the word of*
> *His power, when He had by Himself*
> *purged our sins, **sat down at the***
> ***right hand of the Majesty on***
> ***high**," Hebrews 1:2-3.*

The point of this chapter is to see Jesus. I mean really see Him as He is. He is the purpose of this book, and the purpose of the Holy Bible. We do not read or study the Word of God to have a better life. We do not study the Bible to know the future. We do not study to know ourselves better or to find eternal life. We study the Bible to know Jesus. And in Jesus we find everything else. In Jesus, we find a better life. In Jesus we find ourselves. In Jesus we have a future. In Jesus we have eternal life. **Because Jesus is everything**.

Key Subjects
of the Book of Revelation
with Connections to the Old Testament

What follows is a compilation of most of the key subjects in Revelation. It is not all-inclusive, I know. But it does connect most of Revelation to the Old Testament. I believe the Word of God is never ending in its value or in its interpretations. I believe a person could spend eternity studying from Genesis to Revelation and never fully grasp all the connections. Just *The Language* (Hebrew) alone is three layers deep: mathematically, pictorially, and literally. And if you add to that **all of the ways it connects to Jesus,** you'll have unlimited possible studies. Please! Take your time as you go through these next chapters and have your own Holy Bible open to confirm what you read.

Chapter 11: Letters to His People

"I am the Alpha and the Omega, the First and the Last," and, "What you see, write in a book and send it to the seven churches." Revelation 1:11

Revelation chapters 1–3 are consistent with the Bible's *Big Picture*. What do we call most of the writings in the New Testament? Letters. We have Paul's letters to the churches, Peter's letters to the churches, and so forth. The God of all Scripture has always called His people into holiness through letters or books written by His servants. All the admonishments and encouragements of the seven letters in Revelation are worded with Old Testament language for a reason: Jesus is the same yesterday, today and forever and His message to us, His bride, reflects His faithfulness and never changing character. Notice *The Language:*

Revelation 2:21 "And I gave her time to repent of her sexual immorality, and she did not repent. 22 Indeed I will cast her into a sickbed, and those who commit adultery with her into great *tribulation, unless they repent of their deeds. 23 I will kill her children with death, and all the churches shall know that **I am He** who **searches the minds and hearts. And I will give to each one of you according to your works.**"*

<u>Compared to</u>

*Jeremiah 17:**9** "The heart is deceitful above all things,and desperately wicked; Who can know it? **10 "I, the Lord, search the heart, I test the mind, even to give every man according to his ways, according to the fruit of his doings.**"*

Do you see the language matching up? If you do, then you also understand that Jesus is claiming to be the God of Jeremiah, *'who searches the heart, and tests the mind'.*

One of the things that hits me the hardest in the seven letters to the churches of Revelation is the call to repentance **IN THE CHURCHES.** The passage below is not to the outside world. We often hear it preached at the end of a sermon as a call to unbelievers, and sadly, I believe, more often than not, we dismiss it.

> *Revelation 3:19 "As many as I love, I rebuke and chasten. Therefore be zealous and **repent. 20 Behold, I stand at the door and knock. If anyone hears My voice and opens the door, I will come in to him and dine with him, and he with Me.** 21 To him who overcomes I will grant to sit with Me on My throne, as I also overcame and sat down with My Father on His throne. 22 "He who has an ear, let him hear what the Spirit says to the churches." ' "*

This is a warning to all of us. The Bible, in both Old and New Testaments, directly confronts false worship. And we are not talking about people who worship pagan gods. Those people could care less what Jesus says. The false worship being addressed by Scripture is none other than the false worship of the Lord God and His Messiah, Jesus.

I can't think of one Old Testament book that does not directly confront false worship -- **in the**

church, in 'God's people'! Doesn't Jesus Himself warn us that on that Day many people will say "Lord, Lord..." to which Jesus will reply "depart from Me, you workers of iniquity, I never knew you". This is a warning, a call to us, to make sure we worship "God in spirit and in truth".

*"But the hour is coming, and now is, when the **true worshipers will worship the Father in spirit and truth**; for the Father is seeking such to worship Him. God is Spirit, and those who **worship Him must worship in spirit and truth**." The woman said to Him, "I know that Messiah is coming" (who is called Christ). "When He comes, He will tell us all things." **Jesus said to her, "I who speak to you am He**." John 4:23-26."*

Can you imagine the level of self hate one would bear for eternity having sat in a church their whole life, heard the words of Jesus, and never made it personal? The Apostle James said it like this:

James 1:21-26 "Therefore lay aside all filthiness and overflow of *wickedness, and **receive with meekness the implanted word,** which is able to save your souls. **But be doers of the word, and not hearers only, deceiving yourselves.** For if anyone is a hearer of the word and not a doer, he is like a man observing his natural face in a mirror; for he observes himself, goes away, and immediately forgets what kind of man he was. But he who looks into the perfect law of liberty and continues in it, and is not a forgetful hearer but a doer of the work, this one will be blessed in what he does. If anyone among you thinks he is religious, and does not bridle his tongue but **deceives his own heart, this one's religion is useless."***

If you're curious about true worship vs. false worship, simply ask yourself, who's the focus of my worship? Is it me? Am I more concerned with what I get from worship? Or am I focused on how worshiping makes me feel? Or, is the Lord God our focus? And do we focus on how our worship and obedience makes Him feel? Is His Kingdom the one we are working to build, or are we trying to use Him to build our kingdom? Let's make sure that we are worshiping the Lord

God in truth and spirit, and together, let's build the Kingdom of Jesus Christ.

- Big Questions: What about those promises in the seven letters 'to those who endure to the end'? Do we see God's promises to the Old Testament believer for holding fast to His Word? What about Deuteronomy 28? Does that sound like the prosperity gospel? Or is Jesus a rewarder of the diligent and obedient? What do you think?

Chapter 12: The Throne Room of Heaven

"I watched till thrones were put in place, and the Ancient of Days was seated; **His garment was white as snow, and the hair of His head was like pure wool.** *His throne was a fiery flame, its wheels a burning fire;" Daniel 7:9*

Compare to:

"One like the Son of Man, **clothed with a garment down to the feet** *and girded about the chest with a golden band.* **His head and hair were white like wool, as white as snow**, *and His eyes like a flame of fire;" Revelation 1:13-14.*

Jesus is the Ancient of Days in Daniel 7. And in those verses, Jesus sits on the vacant throne of Man in heaven's throne room. The Big Picture here is big, really big. From all the texts in the Bible, which include Ezekiel, I Kings 22, and others, the throne room of heaven must be absolutely massive. According to Daniel's account ten thousand times ten thousand ministers to the King, which means the square footage must be insanely huge. Imagine the court of Daniel 7, and add to that a place for the four living creatures, plus the thrones of the 24 elders, plus the items of the original Tabernacle from which the earthly tabernacle copied, plus all the saints of both the old *and* new testaments, and the ability to imagine it all in one place becomes overwhelming.

And we have some really neat connections from the Old Testament to confirm what the Apostle John saw while in the throne room.

> *Revelation 4:6 "Before the* **throne there was a sea of glass, like crystal**. *And in the midst of the throne, and around the throne, were four living creatures full of eyes in front and in back."*

Compared to:

> *Exodus 24:9-11. "Then Moses went up, also Aaron, Nadab, and Abihu, and seventy of the elders of Israel, and* **they saw the God of Israel. And there was under His**

89

feet as it were a paved work of sapphire stone, and it was like the very heavens in its clarity. But on the nobles of the children of Israel He did not lay His hand. So they saw God, and they ate and drank.".

- Big Question: How many throne room descriptions can you find in the Old Testament? How do they compare to or add to your understanding of the Throne Room of Revelation?

Chapter 13: The Four Living Creatures

"I saw the Lord sitting on a throne, high and lifted up, and the train of His robe filled the temple. Above it stood seraphim; **each one had six wings**: *with two he covered his face, with two he covered his feet, and with two he flew. And one cried to another and said:*

> **"Holy, holy, holy is the Lord of hosts;**
> *The whole earth is full of His glory!"*
> *Isaiah 6: 1-3*

Compare to:

*Revelation 4: 8. "**The four living creatures, each having six wings,** were full of eyes around and within. And they do not rest day or night, saying:*
> **"Holy, holy, holy,**
> **Lord God Almighty,**
> *Who was and is and is to come!"*

Do you see the connections from Isaiah 6 to Revelation 4? As we go through the key subjects, we will try to make these kinds of connections on each topic.

John saw four living creatures before the throne: a creature like a lion, a creature like a calf, a creature with the face of a man, and a creature like a flying eagle. Believe it or not, these four creatures are part of *The Big Picture* of Scripture. If you're familiar with jewish history, the insignias for the four camps around the tabernacle of the wilderness in Numbers chapter 2, were the same four creatures. Judah's insignia was a lion , Reuben's a man, Ephraim's an ox and Dan's an eagle. Each of these could symbolize the New Testament gospels. I've heard authors connect Matthew with 'the Lion' (showing Jesus as the King of the tribe of Judah), Mark with 'the Ox' (showing Jesus as the servant), Luke with 'the Man' (showing Jesus is the Son of Man) and John with 'the Eagle' (showing Jesus to be God). If you want to take some time and look online, I'm confident you'll find dozens of sermons on these four living creatures from both the Old and New Testaments. *The Language* connections are pretty easy to line up.

> *Revelation 4:7 "The first living creature was **like a lion**, the second living creature **like a calf**, the third*

*living creature had a face **like a man**, and the fourth living creature was **like a flying eagle**. 8 The four living creatures, each having six wings, were full of eyes around and within."*

Compared to

*Ezekiel 1:10 "As for the likeness of their faces, each had the **face of a man**; each of the four had the **face of a lion** on the right side, each of the four had the **face of an ox** on the left side, and each of the four had the **face of an eagle**. 11 Thus were their faces."*

- Big Question: How many wings did Ezekiel's creatures have? Where else can we find these four creatures? Have you ever wondered why these creatures cry "Holy, Holy, Holy" day and night without ceasing? Why do you think Jesus created them?

Chapter 14: The Scroll

*Jeremiah 32:9-15. "So I bought the field from Hanamel, the son of my uncle who was in Anathoth, and weighed out the money—seventeen shekels of silver. And **I signed the deed and sealed it**, took witnesses, and weighed the money on the scales. So I took the purchase deed, **both that which was sealed according to the law and custom, and that which was open;** and I gave the purchase deed to Baruch the son of Neriah, son of Mahseiah, in the presence of Hanamel my uncle's son, and in the presence of the witnesses who signed the purchase deed, before all the Jews who sat in the court of the prison. "Then I charged Baruch before them, saying, 'Thus says the Lord of hosts, the God of Israel: **"Take these deeds, both this purchase deed which is sealed and this deed which is open,** and put them in an earthen* *vessel, that they may last many days."*

Did you catch that? There are two scrolls. One scroll was given to the landowner *'which is open'* and a second scroll which was *'sealed'*. Here's why, and we can see this today. Often, the claim to a piece of land becomes contested. Maybe by a forgery of the title, maybe by a dispute, but the ownership of property can be contested. The ancient world had a way of keeping records. The first scroll would go home with the landowner. He could carry it with him for whatever needs he had. Now, just in case a dispute arose over the *'open'* scroll, then those contesting the title could return to the courts where the second scroll was kept. The *'sealed'* scroll would have unbroken seals as proof of incorruption. Then, and only then, in the presence of the court, would those seals be broken and the true owner of the title would be revealed.

What's *the Big Picture?* Jesus is the Maker and Creator of all things. "For by Him all things were created" Colossians 1: 16. Now in Genesis we know the Creator gave Adam dominion over Earth. Then we read of Satan's deception and man's fall. Somewhere, somehow, through this fall, Satan believes he has the right to Earth. He didn't create it, he didn't earn it, he didn't pay for it, in fact all he has ever done is try to destroy it, but yet he lays claim to Earth. The ownership of Earth is under dispute. And this is why we see a sealed scroll in Revelation chapter 5. It's the title deed for Earth. Which makes sense when you remember that Revelation chapter 4 is the courtroom of Heaven. It's easy sometimes to just see a chapter at a time, but context is always important. The Court of Heaven is in session when we see the scroll presented.

And notice *The Language* surrounding the scroll in Revelation 5:8-10. It is redemption and restoration.

> **"Now when He had taken the scroll**, *the four living creatures and the twenty-four elders fell down before the Lamb, each having a harp, and golden bowls full of incense, which are the prayers of the saints. And they sang a new song, saying:*
>
> *"You are worthy to take the scroll, And to open its seals;* **For You were slain, And have redeemed us to God by Your blood** *Out of every tribe and tongue and people and nation,* **And have made us kings and priests to our God; And we shall reign on the earth."**

The scroll is sealed. This is proof of incorruption. And now, in the presence of witnesses, in the court of Heaven, and before the throne of Almighty God, it is about to be opened, revealing the true Kingship and Lordship of all.

I was helping a new pastor in Guatemala at a newly planted church. I had just received a donation for $200, which I needed badly, as I was low on my funds. But the same day I received the donation, the pastor and I went to a phone store to find a new phone for him. To this day, I am still unsure how he had planned on buying a new phone and getting the service on it because once there, he turned to me and asked to borrow $200. To be honest, in my heart, I was not happy, even though I handed over the money. In fact, I sat down and started pouting privately to Jesus.

"Lord Jesus, for real? I just got that donation. And You know I'm struggling". Then, out of nowhere, an older white man was standing beside me. If you noticed I mentioned he was white. That's because we were in Guatemala, so the two of us kind of stood out.

"Do you mind if I sit here?" he asked. I gestured to the seat, and he sat down. After a couple minutes, he leaned over and asked if I was a Christian because I was wearing a 'Jesus' t-shirt.

"Do you want to know what the Holy Spirit showed me today in my devotions?" he asked.

Ok, no matter how mad I was, that question hooked me.

"Ok, what do you have?" I asked.

"Lordship and Kingship" he said. "I was praying over the title 'King of Kings and Lord of Lords', and this is what the Lord gave me. He's the King of all kings. A king is the final authority in a kingdom. So if He is the 'King of kings' then He has all the authority.

I felt like I already knew that part. But the next part is what blew my mind.

"But 'the Lord of Lords" he continued "is something that took me more time to think about. You see, the 'lord of a manor' has the ownership of the manor. A 'landlord' has ownership of the land. So when the Bible declares Jesus to be 'Lord of lords' what it's saying is that Jesus has ownership of everything, He's the owner of it all. Everything belongs to Him".

At this point, the older gentlemen stood up, shook my hand and walked off. I have never seen him again. Perhaps he was an angel giving me the perfect message that day, because it changed my heart instantly. If Jesus is indeed 'Lord of everything' then what's the big deal about a $200 gift? He'll take care of me and I can trust Him. After all, who's more generous than Jesus? Who's given us this wonderful world? Who's given us food and clothes? And who's given us salvation and an eternal inheritance? Though sometimes I foolishly doubt Him, all I need to do is remind myself of His generosity, and my salvation which came at the expense of His Own Blood (Act 20:28). He didn't have to give us His Word written down and make it available to us. He didn't have to give us two testaments, old and new. He didn't have to give us 66 books if your protestant or 73 if your catholic. And He most definitely didn't have to give us His Son, the greatest gift of all. He did all of this, plus so much more, just because He is generous!

So Jesus is 'King of Kings and Lord of Lords'. And as the Lord of Heaven and Earth, Jesus gets the final say in the affairs of mankind. The book of Revelation is the re-establishment of Lordship despite man's will. As He taught us to pray "May Your will be done on Earth as it is in Heaven".

> Romans 5:14 "Nevertheless death reigned from Adam to Moses, even over those who had not sinned according to the likeness of the transgression of Adam, who is a type of Him who was to come. 15 But the free gift is not like the offense. For if by the one man's offense many died, much more the grace of God and the gift by the grace of the one Man, Jesus Christ, abounded to many. 16 And the gift is not like that which came through the one who sinned. For the judgment which

came from one offense resulted in condemnation, but the free gift which came from many offenses resulted in justification. 17 **For if by the one man's offense death reigned** *through the one,* **much more those who receive the abundance of grace and of the gift of righteousness will reign in life through the One, Jesus Christ.**

- Big Question: Why was only Jesus 'worthy to open the scroll'? Do you think it is because Jesus is the 'Judge of Mankind' (John 5:22) or because of something else?

Chapter 15: The Seven Seals

"The whole vision has become to you like the words of a scroll that is sealed, which men deliver to one who is literate, saying, "Read this, please." And he says, "I cannot, for it is sealed." Isaiah 29:11

What's *The Big Picture* at this point? We are opening a sealed scroll in the Throne Room of Heaven. The location of chapters 4–7 is purposeful. The true King sits on the throne in Heaven. That's a throne Satan wanted to sit on. Satan wanted to be in the place of God.

*"How you have fallen from heaven, O Lucifer, son of the morning! How you are cut down to the ground, you who weakened the nations! For you have said in your heart: 'I will ascend into heaven, **I will exalt my throne above the stars of God**; I will also sit on the mount of the congregation". Isaiah 14:12 & 13.*

But what about the throne of Earth? In Daniel 7, we see thrones being put in place around the throne room of Heaven, but Daniel saw one throne empty. That empty throne was the throne Adam abdicated in the Garden of Eden. That throne is the Throne of Man. Which might explain why Jesus loved to call Himself 'the Son of Man'. That empty throne of Man is for Man, according to the will of God. And that's why we see Jesus as the new and better Adam in Romans. It is Jesus, the Son of Man, God in the flesh– of man, who sits on that throne now. With His blood He purchased man's redemption. WIth His resurrection, He restored mankind back into the will of the Father. Mankind now has dominion again, over the Earth, as co-heirs in Jesus.

Chapters	
1-3	**The Church on Earth**
4-7	**True Kingship & Lordship**
7-9	**7 Trumpets**
10-11	**Testimony of Jesus**
11:15-19	**Jesus is King of Kings**
12-15	**Testimony of Satan**
16	**7 Bowls**
17-19	**False Kingship & Lordship**
20-21	**The Church in Eternity**

In Revelation 6, we are going to see Jesus break open the seven seals on the scroll as proof of two things: 1)True Kingship and 2)True Lordship. If you look at *The Chiasm*, this is the section of True Kingship and Lordship.The chiasm will pair this section with its opposite section, The False Kingship and Lordship of Satan, in chapters 17-20. If you find anything confusing in chapters 17-20, try comparing these two sections.

The breaking of the seals is almost like hitting a reset button on the existing ownership of Earth. Try to picture each seal as a symbol of some type of authority or ownership. And then watch the reaction on Earth, by Satan and his followers. The key here is to listen to *The Language*. It will be reminiscent of Genesis and the creation story. The true title deed of creation is held by Jesus, our Creator. But we are fully aware that Satan lays claim to Earth. Satan has held sway over the will of sinful men for far too long. But this is a story with redemption and restoration. That's why this scroll is being opened, and the true kingship and lordship of Earth is being validated in the court of heaven before the throne.

Let's walk through these seven seals individually. I acknowledge, there are other teachers who have different interpretations for each of these seals, and I am 'ok' with that. I want to encourage you to keep an open mind. If you disagree with me, great! The strength of Christian fellowship is in hearing different interpretations and giving grace to each other. None of us know it all. And none of us are saved by our knowledge. We are saved by faith, and brought to the knowledge of Jesus Christ through patience, diligence, discipleship, and love, in His Holy Spirit. So let's move on to the seals.

The breaking of the <u>First Seal</u> brings a reaction on earth. A conqueror goes out conquering. Now, by command of the Creator all the dominion of Earth was given to Adam. But we have in Jesus a better 'Adam', a Perfect 'Adam'. This is the restoration of man's dominion over Earth through our Redeemer. The reaction on Earth however; is Satan's last grasp for total dominion on Earth. It's a final act of rebellion. Imagine you own a house. Now imagine a squatter has taken over your house and laid claim to it. Imagine you showing up to that house with an officer of the court, title in hand. You will probably get some kind of reaction. The seals broken are proof of Jesus's rightful Kingship and Lordship of Earth, but what John records for us, is the <u>reaction</u> on Earth. Satan is an illegal squatter. And the Book of Revelation is eviction day.

In reaction to the <u>Second Seal</u> being broken open, peace is taken from earth. Peace was present in the Garden of Eden until sin entered in. And only when Jesus sits as King of Earth on Earth, will He restore peace.

My brother Chris, is a pastor serving the Navy's brig in Charleston, South Carolina. He likes to bring up the Peace of Jesus when discussing Jesus as God. He often has Muslim, Mormon, and Jehovah's Witnesses in his services. Jesus told his disciples "Peace I leave with you, **My peace I give to you**". Only God is the source of peace so only He can give peace, therefore, Jesus is God in the flesh. And only the true God can give true peace to mankind.

The <u>Third Seal</u> is broken and justice is taken away. In the Garden, with the entry of sin also came the wages of sin, which is death. When the third seal is broken, suddenly the wages of man's labor aren't enough to feed him. "*A quart of wheat for a denarius*", (Rev. 6:6.). A denarius was anywhere from one week's labor to three week's labor, depending on your source. Here's a way to picture this: a quart of flour is 4 cups of flour, and that makes an average loaf of bread. So when we see "*a quart of wheat for a denarius*", it is like saying a week of work for a loaf of bread. That's telling us, during the great tribulation, the wages of a man won't be enough to feed him. The average man will not be able to work for his daily bread. Can you imagine working for a week, or two, in exchange for a single loaf of bread? Yet the King of Heaven tells us to pray, and to simply ask Him *'to give us this day our daily bread'*. The Lord has, and always will, provide for His people.

> *Isaiah 33: 15-16, "Who among us shall dwell with the devouring fire? Who among us shall dwell with everlasting burnings?" He who walks righteously and speaks uprightly, He who despises the gain of oppressions, Who gestures with his hands, refusing bribes, Who stops his ears from hearing of bloodshed, And shuts his eyes from seeing evil: He will dwell on high; His place of defense will be the fortress of rocks;* **Bread will be given him, His water will be sure.***"*

The <u>Fourth Seal</u> brings Death and Hades. God told Adam 'Dying you shall die', but the first gospel message was also given in Genesis 3, that God would send a Promised One through the *'Seed of the Woman'*. This is redemption and restoration. Did you know the promise of eternal life was given to man before creation?

> *"in hope of eternal life which God, who cannot lie, promised before time began". Titus 1:2*

In Revelation, we see a lot of death. There's death in breaking of the seals. there's death in the seven trumpets. But for those of us in Jesus, death holds no power. And did you know that Satan is not the ruler over hell? The Bible tells us that Satan is the most punished one in hell. Jesus is the ruler over hell, and Jesus has the power and authority over death. The fourth seal is not about kingship or authority of Satan, but it reveals the true kingship and lordship of Jesus Christ.

> *Revelation 6: 9-11, "When He opened the Fifth Seal, I saw under the altar the souls of those who had been slain for the word of God and for the testimony which they held. And they cried with a loud voice, saying, "**How long, O Lord**, holy and true, until You judge and avenge*

our blood on those who dwell on the earth?" Then a white robe was given to each of them; and it was said to them that they should rest a little while longer, until both the number of their fellow servants and their brethren, who would be killed as they were, was completed."

Let's examine the fifth seal. Because this seal, and its response is only seen in Heaven. The fifth seal is heaven's response to the killing of the saints on Earth. Does *The Language* here sound familiar: **"How long O Lord"**? If you search those exact words you'll find it a lot in the Old Testament. Here's a couple examples:

*Isaiah 6:11-12: Then I said, "**Lord, how long?**" And He answered: "Until the cities are laid waste and without inhabitant, The houses are without a man, The land is utterly desolate,"*

*Psalms 13:1 "**How long, O Lord?** Will You forget me forever?"*

*Habakkuk 1:2 "**O Lord, how long** shall I cry, And You will not hear?*

Even cry out to You, "Violence!" And
You will not save."

If you want to see the reaction to the fifth seal on Earth, use *The Chiasm* to look at the opposite correlating section, which is 'False Kingship and Lordship' in chapters 15-17. There you'll see that despite the signs and wonders from Heaven, the men of Earth *"blaspheme the God of heaven and do not repent from their sins.",* (Rev.16:11) The ungodly double down on their position of rebellion.

I think the biggest contrast between the martyrs of Jesus and the ungodly of Satan is **hope**. Those in Jesus have *hope* of the resurrection to Life. We have *hope* of restoration and redemption. We have the *hope* of resurrection to a life better because of Jesus! But those bound to Satan have no *hope* in life, and no *hope* in Death.

The Sixth Seal is a sign in the heavens. Can we remember an Old Testament sign set in the heavens? In the Days of Noah? God made a promise to Noah, and confirmed it in the heavens with the sign of a rainbow. Now, just as Jesus promised, before His return, it would be as *'in the Days of Noah'* (Matthew 24). There is a sign given in the heavens with the breaking of the Sixth Seal.

"The sun darkens, the moon becomes like blood, and the stars of heaven fall to the Earth". Just as the rainbow brought hope to the believer, in contrast, this sign brings despair to the unbeliever.

> *"Fall on us and hide us from the face of Him who sits on the throne and from the wrath of the Lamb! For the great day of His wrath has come, and who is able to stand?" Revelation 6:16-17.*

The <u>Seventh Seal</u> calls forward the *Israel of God* (Gal. 6:16). This is a call to all those who are the 'sons of Abraham by faith'. The next chapter will go deeper into the 144,000, but the takeaway here is simple, these are God's Inheritance.

> *"Blessed are the meek, for* **they shall inherit the Earth**, *Matthew 5:5*

And
> *"For this you know, that no fornicator, unclean person, nor covetous man, who is an idolater,*

has any inheritance in the
kingdom of Christ and God",
Ephesians 5:5, (1 Cor. 6:9, Galatians
5:19-21.)

The Seventh Seal is the authority of King Jesus to give his inheritance to whomever He chooses. I love matching *The Language* here to one of my favorite Old Testament passages:

> *"Remember the days of old, consider the years of many generations. Ask your father, and he will show you; Your elders, and they will tell you:* ***When the Most High divided their inheritance to the nations***, *when He separated the sons of Adam, He set the boundaries of the peoples according to the number of the children of Israel. For* ***the Lord's portion is His people; Jacob is the place of His inheritance.***" *Deuteronomy 32: 7-9.*

- Big Question: If You owned something and someone else claimed it, how would you validate your ownership? Why do you think Heaven has a courtroom with such proceedings? Does God's due process of law and order reveal anything to you about His Nature and Character?

Chapter 16: Two different 144,000

     To begin with, it is important to note, there are two mentions of 144,00 in the Book of Revelation. If you are getting familiar with *The Chiasm*, you would expect this. Right? If you have 144,000 mentioned on one side of the chiasm, you should expect it on the other side. And again, the great thing about this tool is that it allows Scripture to give us Scriptures' interpretation.

     But before we begin this chapter, I want to remind the readers of what I said in the introduction. I am not trying to tell you what to think, but teaching you how to understand what you see in the text. You are free to disagree with me here. So put your thinking caps on and get prepared to do some real research here.

     The First 144,000.

     The <u>Seventh Seal</u> calls forward the '*Israel of God*' (Gal. 6:16). This is a call to all those who are the sons of Abraham **by faith**. In Revelation 7:4, John <u>hears</u> a roll call of 144,000 Israelites, but in verse 9, he turns to <u>see</u> something completely different. In verse 9, John <u>sees</u> something that doesn't match what he heard. He sees a multitude of every tribe, nation, tongue, which couldn't be numbered. These two things are purposely made to contradict each other. First, you can't have **144,000** be **numberless**, those two descriptions contradict each other. And secondly, you can't have **Israelites** being **every nation, tribe, and tongue,** those two descriptions also contradict themselves . So let's ask ourselves, 'what is going on here?'.

For another example of Scripture interpreting Scripture, chapter one gives us a matching example. The example in chapter one matches the same formula for this text. John will <u>hear</u> one thing, then turn to <u>see</u> another thing. Can you see the difference below?

> *"I was in the Spirit on the Lord's Day, and **I heard** behind me a loud voice, as of a trumpet, saying, "I am the Alpha and the Omega, the First and the Last," and, "What you see, write in a book and send it to the seven churches which are in Asia: to Ephesus, to Smyrna, to Pergamos, to Thyatira, to Sardis, to Philadelphia, and to Laodicea." Then I turned **to see** the voice that spoke with me. **And having turned I saw** seven golden lampstands, and in the midst of the seven lampstands One like the Son of Man," Revelation 1:10-13*

John hears the authority of **The Father**, (Isa. 44:6,) but turns to see who? The Son of Man,

Jesus. Why? Because we have One God. The text gives us understanding. John <u>hears</u> one thing, but turns to <u>see</u> *the understanding of it*. John hears something he thinks he knows all about, but in turning to see, **his understanding becomes clearer**. This example in chapter one is not coincidental. When we see the exact same **Language** pop up in chapter seven, our reflexes should kick in. If John <u>hears</u> one thing and then turns to <u>see</u> another, we should slow down and pay attention to the text because it is about to make our understanding clearer.

Look at *The Language* for context. John gives us a list of 12 tribes, so let's go back to the Old Testament to find a list of the 12 Tribes.

Genesis 29-30 gives us a list of Jacob's sons: **Reuben, Simeon, Levi, Judah, Dan, Naphtali, Gad, Asher, Issachar, Zebulun, Joseph, and Benjamin**. Take a minute here. If your Holy Bible is not yet open to Revelation chapter 7, do so now. And compare. Does John's list of Tribes match up with Genesis? **No it does not**. What names are different? What names are missing? And what does this mean?

Let's explain a couple things about the Twelve Tribes and the typical listings we are used to. First, Levi is not supposed to be mentioned. The tribe of Levi is the Lord's Portion

(Deuteronomy 10:9). Second, Joseph is typically not mentioned in the lists of the tribes because he was given a double portion through his two sons, and they are usually mentioned: Manasseh and Ephriam. If you want to see the math on this, start with twelve, the twelve sons of Jacob. Now subtract Levi (12-1=11), and subtract Joseph (11-1=10), and add back in Joseph's two sons (10+2=12). Twelve tribes.

But that still doesn't explain why we have a different list in Revelation 7, does it? Who is missing? Ephriam and Dan? Well, if you are familiar with the Old Testament, both of these tribes lead Israel into Idolatry. Feel free to research the history of those two tribes. Can you see Manasseh in verse 6 and his father, Joseph, in verse 8? These would be clues. The list we have in Revelation chapter 7 seems put together, seems forced, to have twelve names in it. At this point, you could easily make an argument that this list is metaphorical because it can't be literal. So why even include it? That is why we see the text gives us understanding. As the text goes on, John turns to <u>see</u> something different than what he <u>heard</u>.

Do we see any clues in *The Language* prior to the list? Look back in the text.

*"till we have **sealed the servants of our God on their foreheads**." And I heard the number of those **who were sealed**. Revelation 7: 3-4*

The Apostle Pauls wrote:

*"In Him you also trusted, after you heard the word of truth, the gospel of your salvation; in whom also, having believed, **you were sealed** with the Holy Spirit of promise, **who is the guarantee of our inheritance** until the redemption of the purchased possession, to the praise of His glory." Ephesians 1:13-14.*

Those called forward are **sealed on their foreheads** with a mark. Four times we see God's people being sealed with a mark on their foreheads. (We also cover this in chapter 19: The Mark on the Forehead, Rev. 7: 3, Rev. 9:4, Rev. 14:1, & Rev. 22:5).

*2 Corinthians 1:21-22. "Now He who establishes us with you in Christ and has anointed us is God, who also **has sealed us** and given*

us the Spirit in our hearts as a
guarantee."

And here's an Old Testament
connection:

> Ezekiel 9:4. "The Lord said to
> him, "Go through the midst of the
> city, through the midst of Jerusalem,
> and put a **mark on the foreheads**
> of the men who sigh and cry over all
> the abominations that are done
> within it."

In both the Old and New Testaments,
God spiritually marks His people. He seals
them as a sign as His inheritance. The first
144,000 of Revelation 7, are the sealed
inheritance of The Lord God.
The Second 144,000.
Now that we are familiar with the chiastic
structure, we should be looking for the second
144,000 in the other half of Revelation, right?

> Revelation 14:1 "Then I looked,
> and behold, a Lamb standing on
> Mount Zion, and with Him **one
> hundred and forty-four
> thousand,** having **His Father's
> name written on their
> foreheads.** And I heard a voice

*from heaven, like the voice of many waters, and like the voice of loud thunder. And I heard the sound of harpists playing their harps. They sang as it were a new song before the throne, before the four living creatures, and the elders; and no one could learn that song except **the hundred and forty-four thousand** who were <u>redeemed from the earth</u>. These are the ones who were not defiled with women, for they are virgins. These are the ones who follow the Lamb wherever He goes. <u>These were redeemed from among men,</u> being <u>firstfruits</u> to God and to the Lamb. And in their mouth was found <u>no deceit</u>, for they are without fault before the throne of God." Revelation 14:1-5.*

The Language is completely different for this 144,000. What are some of the things that describe this group? *"They are redeemed from Earth"*- what does that mean to you? Or, *"they are redeemed from among men"*? How about *"virgins"* or *"in their mouth was found no deceit,"*? Absolutely none of this is found in the First 144,000.

Of course the existence of two sets of 144,000 matches up for *The Chiasm*, but the chiastic structure allows the two sides to either match or to be opposite. Perhaps one side, the first group, is the new Israel of God, which includes the New Testament Church, and the second group is the actual nation of Israel-Jewish believers? What do you think?

Perhaps take a moment to step back and look at *The Big Picture,* and remember that Jesus keeps all of His promises. This could be the evidence that our God is big enough to keep His promises no matter how literal or metaphorical we interpret them.

- Big Question: What differences did you see in the two groups of 144,000? If there are two different groups, does that help your understanding of any Old or New Testament passages?

Chapter 17: The Four Horsemen

In *The Big Picture*, God is supreme. Even though Satan lays claim to Earth, Satan still has to obey the perimeters that God gives him. It's interesting to think of the powers Satan has or is allowed to have.

One example that comes to mind is Satan's control of the weather. In the book of Revelation, the Beast and the False Prophet will be able to bring down fire from Heaven (Rev. 13:13) and work signs that would 'deceive even the elect if possible'. We see this first demonstrated in the Old Testament book of Job. God allows Satan to attack Job and it's captivating to see Satan mimic the power of God, by using the weather.

"While he was still speaking,
*another also came and said, "**The***
***fire of God fell from heaven** and*
burned up the sheep and the

*servants, and consumed them; and I alone have escaped to tell you!"… "Your sons and daughters were eating and drinking wine in their oldest brother's house, and suddenly **a great wind** came from across the wilderness and struck **the four corners of the house**, and it fell on the young people, and they are dead; and I alone have escaped to tell you!" Job 1:16-18*

Did you notice, the surviving servant attributed the fire that burned up the animals as the 'the fire of God'? But it wasn't an act of God. And the wind that struck the house, killing Job's children wasn't from God either. Satan mimics the power of God.

In the book of Revelation, we see the 'god of this world' using great signs and wonders to deceive the world. If we only look at Revelation, and we don't compare it to the Old Testament, then we are stuck only seeing one angle, or viewpoint. But by adding a second angle, or viewpoint, we can gain a better perspective.

Let's see four horsemen in the book of Zechariah, and perhaps they may add to our understanding of the four horsemen of Revelation.

> *"I saw by night, and behold,* **a man riding on a red horse,** *and it stood among the myrtle trees in the hollow; and* **behind him were horses: red, sorrel, and white.** *Then I said, "My lord, what are these?" So the angel who talked with me said to me, "I will show you what they are." And the man who stood among the myrtle trees answered and said,* **"These are the ones whom the LORD has sent to walk to and fro throughout the earth.**" *So they answered the Angel of the LORD, who stood among the myrtle trees, and said, "We have walked to and fro throughout the earth, and behold,* **all the earth is resting quietly.**" *Zechariah 1:8-11*

Let's keep reading into chapter six:

> *"Then I turned and raised my eyes and looked, and behold, four chariots were coming from between two mountains, and the mountains were mountains of bronze. With the*

*first chariot were **red horses**, with the second chariot **black horses**, with the third chariot **white horses**, and with the fourth chariot **dappled horses**—strong steeds. Then I answered and said to the angel who talked with me, "**What are these, my lord?**" And the angel answered and said to me, "**These are four spirits of heaven, who go out from their station before the Lord of all the earth.** The one with the black horses is going to the north country, the white are going after them, and the dappled are going toward the south country." Then the strong steeds went out, eager to go, **that they might walk to and fro throughout the earth.** And He said, "**Go, walk to and fro throughout the earth.**" So they walked to and fro throughout the earth. And He called to me, and spoke to me, saying, "**See, those who go toward the north country have given rest to My Spirit in the north country.**"*
Zechariah 6:1-9

Does this help your understanding? The horsemen of both Zechariah and Revelation match in a couple ways. The colors are similar.

There's four of them. They seem to be either agents of change or observers to Earth. And perhaps, in both books, they are servants of the Lord God. By comparing both Zechariah and Revelation, does this add to your understanding of the Four Horsemen?

- Big Question: Why are the Four Horsemen in the 1st four seals of Revelation 6, but no horsemen for the last three seals?

Chapter 18: The Seven Trumpets

*Joshua 6: 4-5 "**seven priests shall bear seven trumpets** of rams' horns before the ark. But the seventh day you shall march around the city seven times, and **the priests shall blow the trumpets**. It shall come to pass, when they make a long blast with the ram's horn, and when you hear the sound of the trumpet, that all the people shall shout with a great shout; then the wall of the city will fall down flat. And the people shall go up every man straight before him."*

Did you know, following the exodus from Egypt, God's people used seven trumpets in their worship? *The Language* allows us to make a perfect connection here. We know Moses established the tabernacle and worship to reflect what God had shown him on the mountain. So, is it reasonable to conclude that the Israelites had seven priests carrying seven trumpets because that's what Moses saw in Heaven?

For context, Joshua's victory over Jericho was about 40 years after the Tabernacle of the Wilderness was built. I added this because if you have the opportunity to study the "feast of trumpets", the history is very vague. Somehow this feast has morphed through the years. It seems to have had different meanings and traditions through different periods of time. I believe it is important to know that from the beginning, the original worship, immediately following the exodus, involved seven trumpets.

> *Revelation 8:1-6 "When He opened the seventh seal, there was silence in heaven for about half an hour. 2 **And I saw the seven angels who stand before God, and to them were given seven trumpets.** 3 Then another angel, having a golden censer, came and stood at the altar. He was given much incense, that he should offer it with the prayers of all the saints upon the golden altar which was before the throne. 4 And the smoke*

of the incense, with the prayers of the saints, ascended before God from the angel's hand. 5 Then the angel took the censer, filled it with fire from the altar, and threw it to the earth. And there were noises, thunderings, lightnings, and an earthquake. 6 **So the seven angels who had the seven trumpets** *prepared themselves to sound."*

By the way, did you see the *Chiasm* in the passage above?

D) Seven angels with seven trumpets (8:2)

C)   Angel with a censer at the altar (8:3)

B)   Prayers of the saints (8:3)

Apex)   Before the Throne (8:3)

B)   Prayers of the saints (8:4)

C)   Angel with a censer at the altar (8:5)

D) Seven angels with seven trumpets (8:6)

We are about half way through this book, and I'm hoping your skills of using the three tools is getting better and better. In the bigger chiasm of Revelation, these seven trumpets match up with the seven bowls.

7 Trumpets		7 Bowls
1. Vegetation Struck (8:7)		1. Sores on Mankind (16:2)
2. Seas Struck (8:8)		2. Sea turns to Blood (16:3)
3. Water Struck (8:10)		3. Water turns to Blood (16:4)
4. Sun, Moon, Stars Struck (8:12)		4. Sun scorches Mankind (16:8)
5. Locust Army, pain (9:1)		5. Darkness, pain and sores (16:10)
6. Euphrates, 4 angels (9:13)		6. Euphrates, demonic miracles (16:12)
7. Great earthquake & hail (11:19)		7. Great earthquake & hail (16:18, 20)

Let's ask ourselves a question: Who is blowing the trumpets and who is doing the destruction on earth? Maybe *the Language* of the Old Testament can help us understand a little bit more. *Joel 2:1-11*:

Joel 2:1-11, **"Blow the trumpet in Zion, and sound an alarm in My holy mountain!** *Let all the inhabitants of the land tremble; For the day of the LORD is coming, For it is at hand: a day of darkness and gloominess, a day of clouds and thick darkness, Like the morning clouds spread over the mountains.* **A people come, great and strong, The like of whom has never been; nor will there ever be any such after them,** *Even for many successive generations. A fire devours before them, and behind them a flame burns; The land is like the Garden of Eden before them, And behind them a desolate wilderness; surely nothing shall escape them.* **Their appearance is like the appearance of horses***; and like swift steeds, so they run.*

With a noise like chariots over
mountaintops they leap,
Like the noise of a flaming fire that
devours the stubble, like a strong
people set in battle array.

Before them the people writhe in
pain; all faces are drained of color.
They run like mighty men, they
climb the wall like men of war;
Every one marches in formation,
and they do not break ranks.

They do not push one another; every one
marches in his own column.
Though they lunge between the weapons,
they are not cut down.
They run to and fro in the city,
They run on the wall; they climb into the
houses,
They enter at the windows **like a thief**.
The earth quakes before them,
the heavens tremble;
**The sun and moon grow dark,
and the stars diminish their
brightness.**
**The Lord gives voice before His
army,**
For His camp is very great;
For strong is the One who executes
His word.
**For the day of the Lord is great
and very terrible; Who can
endure it?**

Or:

> *Ezekiel 33:3-6 "When he sees the sword coming upon the land, if **he blows the trumpet and warns the people,** then **whoever hears the sound of the trumpet and does not take warning,** if the sword comes and takes him away, **his blood shall be on his own head. He heard the sound of the trumpet, but did not take warning; his blood shall be upon himself.** But **he who takes warning will save his life.** But if the watchman sees the sword coming and **does not blow the trumpet,** and the people are not warned, and the sword comes and takes any person from among them, he is taken away in his iniquity; but **his blood I will require at the watchman's hand.'"*

Research how many times the blowing of a trumpet is mentioned in the Old Testament as a warning or for the "Great Day of the Lord". Here's a couple references (Isa. 27.13, Jer. 4:5, Eze. 33:6, Hos 5:8 Joel 2:1, Zech 9:14, Num 29:-6, Ps 81).

Perhaps the trumpets sound from Heaven and are heard on Earth as a warning to be prepared. Or perhaps the trumpets are only heard in Heaven. What do you think?

- Big Question: How did Paul know these seven trumpets would be a foreshadowing of the Day of the Lord? Paul told us that "at the last trumpet... the dead will rise" (1 Cor. 15:52). Does this tell us when the first resurrection will be?

Chapter 19: The Mark on the Forehead

Ezekiel 9:1-11 "Then He called out in my hearing with a loud voice, saying, "Let those who have charge over the city draw near, each with a deadly weapon in his hand." And suddenly six men came from the direction of the upper gate, which faces north, each with his battle-axe in his hand. One man among them was clothed with linen and had a writer's inkhorn at his side. They went in and stood beside the bronze altar. Now the glory of the God of Israel had gone up from the cherub, where it had been, to the threshold of the temple. And He called to the man clothed with linen, who had the writer's inkhorn at his side; and the LORD said to him, "Go through the midst of the city, through the midst of Jerusalem, and put a mark on the foreheads of the men who sigh and cry over all the abominations that are done within it." To the others He said in my hearing, "Go after him through the city and kill; do not let your eye spare, nor have any pity. Utterly slay old and young men, maidens and little children and women; but do not come near anyone on whom is the mark; and begin at My sanctuary." *So they began with the elders who were before the temple. Then He said to them, "Defile the temple, and fill the courts with the slain. Go out!" And they went out and killed in the city. So it was, that while they were killing them, I was left alone; and I fell on my face and cried out, and said, "Ah, Lord G*OD*! Will You destroy all the remnant of Israel in pouring out Your fury on Jerusalem?" Then He said to me, "The iniquity of the house of Israel and Judah is exceedingly great, and the land is full of bloodshed, and the city full of perversity; for they say, 'The L*ORD *has forsaken the land, and the L*ORD *does not see!' And as for Me also, My eye will neither spare, nor will I have pity, but I will recompense their deeds on their own head." Just then, the man clothed with linen, who had the inkhorn at his side, reported back and said, "I have done as You commanded me."*

Did you know the people of God have received a mark on their foreheads? Look what the Apostle Paul wrote about the seal of God on believers.

*"Now He who establishes us with you in Christ and has anointed us is God, who also has **sealed us** and given us the Spirit in our hearts as a guarantee." 2 Corinthians 1:22.*

*"In Him you also trusted, after you heard the word of truth, the gospel of your salvation; in whom also, having believed, **you were sealed** with the Holy Spirit of promise, who is the guarantee of our inheritance until the redemption of the purchased possession, to the praise of His glory." Ephesians 1:13-14.*

Now let's ask ourselves, do we see this mark of God in the book of Revelation? Yes, we do.

*Rev 7:3 "saying, "Do not harm the earth, the sea, or the trees **till we have sealed the servants of our God on their foreheads**."*

*Rev. 9:4 "They were commanded **not to harm** the grass of the earth, or any green thing, or any tree, **but only those men who do not have the seal of God on their foreheads**."*

Rev. 14:1 "Then I looked, and behold, a Lamb standing on Mount

*Zion, and with Him one hundred and forty-four thousand, **having His Father's name written on their foreheads.***"

If you're counting, that's three times the book of Revelation, where God's people are marked on their foreheads. And it's **after** we see God's mark on His people three times, we see the mark of the beast mentioned. Satan copycats God by marking his people.

The Book of Revelation also ends, with the saints bearing the mark of the Lord on our foreheads.

*Revelation 22:4, "They shall see His face, **and His name shall be on their foreheads**. There shall be no night there: They need no lamp nor light of the sun, for the Lord God gives them light. And they shall reign forever and ever."*

Here's a cool thing to think about: Satan isn't the god of the spiritual world, he was kicked out of heaven. The Lord God is the God of the spiritual world, and He marks His people with a spiritual mark. Satan is left with only the physical world to fight for, which is why we see him mark his people in the flesh, on their physical bodies. This also explains why he wants mankind to indulge in the physical or fleshy sins. The more a person indulges their physical body, the more they become slave to it. It was submission to Satan's will that left mankind spiritually dead. Satan wants mankind bound, like him, to the physical world. But in Jesus, we are born again, into a spiritual resurrection. Praise and honor, to Our Savior who has made us spiritually alive in Him.

I want to finish this chapter by addressing a specific fear I often hear a lot of christians ask about. Let me say it clearly, **you will not and cannot be tricked into accepting the Mark of the Beast.** The Holy Bible is clear on this. The Mark given by God and the mark given by Satan are directly linked to a clear choice. God's people are not accidentally marked by Him, nor will Satan's people be accidentally marked by him. One must make a clear, conscious decision as to where their allegiance lies before they receive a mark of ownership.

- Big Question: What is the mark of the Beast? Is knowing what the Mark of the Beast is more important than knowing what it controls?

Chapter 20: The Locust Army

Joel 1:1 "Hear this, you elders, and give ear, ... tell your children about it, let your children tell their children, and their children another generation. **What the chewing locust left, the swarming locust has eaten; What the swarming locust left, the crawling locust has eaten; and what the crawling locust left, the consuming locust has eaten.** Awake, you drunkards, and weep; and wail, all you drinkers of wine, because of the new wine, it has been cut off from your mouth. For a nation has come up against My land, Strong, and without number; His **teeth are the teeth of a lion**, And he has the fangs of a fierce lion. He has laid waste My vine, and ruined My fig tree; He has stripped it bare and thrown it away; Its branches are made white. Lament like a virgin girded with sackcloth for the husband of her youth.

The grain offering and the drink offering have been cut off from the house of the Lord; the priests mourn, who minister to the Lord. The field is

*wasted, The land mourns; For the
grain is ruined, The new wine is
dried up, The oil fails. Be ashamed,
you farmers, Wail, you vinedressers,*
for the wheat and the barley;
*Because the harvest of the field has
perished.The vine has dried up, and*
the fig tree *has withered;* **The
pomegranate tree,
The palm tree also, And the
apple tree—
All the trees of the field are
withered;** *Surely joy has withered
away from the sons of men."*

Now notice *The Language* when the description is
given to this invading army in Joel:

**"Their appearance is like the
appearance of horses;**
And like swift steeds, so they run. **With a
noise like chariots"** *Joel 2: 4-5*

So let's <u>compare</u> that to the Locust Army of
Revelation,

*Revelation 9:8, "The shape of
the locusts was* **like horses
prepared for battle.** *On their
heads were crowns of something like
gold, and their faces were like the
faces of men. They had hair like
women's hair, and* **their teeth**

were like lions' teeth And they had breastplates like breastplates of iron, and the sound of their wings was like the sound of chariots with many horses running into battle."

Do you see similarities in *the Language*? In several Old Testament books, The uses an army of locusts for destruction, so the sight of a locust army in Revelations itself is nothing new. Egypts was visited with a Plague of Locusts. (Deut. 28:38, Jdg 6:5, Isa 33:4, Joel 1-2, Nah 3:15-17) Locusts themselves are consumers but not usually consumed, or eaten by us. This could be metaphorical or literal, what do you think?

Some would compare this cloud of locusts to the opposite of the Glory Cloud of the Lord. In the Old Testament, we see the Glory Cloud of God fill His temple, as a symbol of His presence in their worship. Do you think this could be an anti-glory cloud for Satan, as he fills the world with destruction?

- Big Question: Why are there so many connections between Joel and Revelation? Do you think there could be a connection with John the Baptist who came before Christ eating locusts and wild honey?

141

Chapter 21: The Euphrates River

Isaiah 8:7-10, "Behold, the Lord brings up over them, The waters of **the River (Euphrates)**, *strong and mighty— ...He will pass through Judah, He will overflow and pass over."*

Isaiah 11:12-16 **"He will set up a banner for the nations,** *And will assemble the outcasts of Israel, And gather together the dispersed of Judah From* **the four corners of the earth**... *The Lord will utterly destroy the tongue of the Sea of Egypt; With His mighty wind He will shake His fist over* **the River (the Euphrates), And strike it in the seven streams, And make men crossover dry-shod.** *There will be a highway for the remnant of His people Who will be left from Assyria,* **As it was for Israel In the day that he came up from the land of Egypt."**

Compare with the Six Trumpet:

*Revelation 9:14-16, "Release the four angels who are bound at the **great river Euphrates**." So the four angels, who had been prepared for the hour and day and month and year, were released to kill a third of mankind. Now the number of the army of horsemen was two hundred million; I heard the number of them."*

And the Sixth Bowl:

*Revelation 16: 12-16: "Then the sixth angel poured out his bowl on **the great river Euphrates**, and **its water was dried up**, so that **the way of the kings from the east might be prepared**. And I saw three unclean spirits like frogs coming out of the mouth of the dragon, out of the mouth of the beast, and out of the mouth of the false prophet. For they are spirits of demons, performing signs, which go out to the kings of the earth and of the whole world, to gather them to the battle of that great day of God Almighty. **"Behold, I am coming***

143

*as a thief. Blessed is he who watches, and keeps his garments, lest he walk naked and they see his shame." **And they gathered them together to the place** called in Hebrew, **Armageddon.***"

- Big Question? What kept the Euphrates river from drying all these years? Is it a miracle? Why does Jesus repeat **"Behold I come as a thief"** right before the Battle of Armageddon? (Rev. 16:15). Is this a significance to where this reminder is placed?

Chapter 22: Eat The Scroll

*Revelation 10:8, "Then the voice which I heard from heaven spoke to me again and said, "Go, take the little book which is open in the hand of the angel who stands on the sea and on the earth." 9 So I went to the angel and said to him, "Give me the little book." And he said to me, "**Take and eat it**; and it will make your stomach bitter, but it will be as sweet as honey in your mouth." 10 Then I took the little book out of the angel's hand and ate it, and it was **as sweet as honey** in my mouth. But when I had eaten it, my stomach became bitter. 11 And he said to me, "**You must prophesy again about many <u>peoples, nations, tongues, and kings.</u>**"*

<u>Compare to</u>:

*Ezekiel 3: 1 Moreover He said to me, "Son of man, eat what you find; eat this scroll, and go, speak to the house of Israel." 2 So I opened my mouth, and He caused me **to eat that scroll**. 3 He said to me, "Son of man, feed your belly, and fill your stomach with this scroll that I give*

*you." So I ate, and it was **in my mouth like honey in sweetness.** 4 Then He said to me: "Son of man, go to the house of Israel and speak with My words to them. 5 For you are not sent to a people of unfamiliar speech and of hard language, but to* **<u>the house of Israel</u>**,

By the way, do you remember from our chapter on the 144,000, John hears Israelites called, but turns to see a multitude of "nations, tribes, peoples and tongues," (Rev. 7:9). Do you see a similar contrast in the two passages above? (Underlined).

There is a third mention in Scripture, of someone eating the Word of God. There's Ezekiel, John, and below, Jeremiah.

> *Jeremiah 15:16 "**Your words were found, and I ate them,** And Your word was to me the joy and rejoicing of my heart; For I am called by Your name, O Lord God of hosts."*

- Big Question: Are you really what you eat? Are we digesting the Word of God to make it a part of us? How far do we go to make His Holy Bible become part of our very being?

Chapter 23: The Angel Swears to Heaven

Revelation 10:1-7 "I saw still another mighty angel coming down from heaven, clothed with a cloud. And a rainbow was on his head, his face was like the sun, and his feet like pillars of fire. He had a little book open in his hand. And he set his right foot on the sea and his left foot on the land, and cried with a loud voice, as when a lion roars. When he cried out, seven thunders uttered their voices. Now when the seven thunders uttered their voices, I was about to write; but I heard a voice from heaven saying to me, "Seal up the things which the seven thunders uttered, and do not write them." ***The angel whom I saw standing on the sea and on the land raised up his hand to heaven and swore by Him who lives forever and ever, who created heaven and the things that are in it, the earth and the things that are in it, and the sea and the things that are in it, that there should be delay no***

longer, *but in the days of the sounding of the seventh angel, when he is about to sound,* **the mystery of God would be finished,** *as He declared to His servants the prophets."*

Compare to:

> Daniel 12:7 *"Then I heard the man clothed in linen,* **who was above the waters of the river, when he held up his right hand and his left hand to heaven, and swore by Him who lives forever, that it shall be for a time, times, and half a time; and when the power of the holy people has been completely shattered, all these things shall be finished."*

I find these two passages fascinating. *The Language* matches up nicely. *The Big Picture* of Scripture would suggest these two passages could be the same event, with two witnesses. I've always loved Sci-Fi movies, so to me, this could be like a future event with two prophets, Daniel and John, watching the same thing at the same time. I often wonder if this is so, would these two men have been able to see each other. What do you think?

- Big Question: Did Daniel and John witness the same event in time? Did John see the same angel Daniel saw? Is it possible both these men were transported in time and saw the future event together?

Chapter 24: The Beasts

Daniel 7, "In the first year of Belshazzar, king of Babylon, Daniel had a dream and visions of his head while on his bed. Then he wrote down the dream, telling the main facts. 2 Daniel spoke, saying, "I saw in my vision by night, and behold, the four winds of heaven were stirring up the Great Sea. 3 And **four great beasts** came up from the sea, each different from the other. 4 The first was like a lion, and had eagle's wings. I watched till its wings were plucked off; and it was lifted up from the earth and made to stand on two feet like a man, and a man's heart was given to it. 5 "And suddenly another beast, a second, like a bear. It was raised up on one side, and had three ribs in its mouth between its teeth. And they said thus to it: 'Arise, devour much flesh!' 6 "After this I looked, and there was another, like a leopard, which had on its back four wings of a bird. The beast also had four heads, and dominion was given to it. 7 "After this I saw in the night visions, and behold, a fourth beast, dreadful and terrible, exceedingly strong. It had huge iron teeth; it was devouring, breaking in pieces, and trampling the residue with its feet. It was different from all the beasts that were before it, and it had **ten horns**... 15 "I, Daniel, was grieved in my spirit within my body, and the visions of my head troubled me. 16 I came near to one of those who stood by, and asked him the truth of all this. **So he told me and made known to me the interpretation of these things**: 17 'Those great beasts, which are four, are four kings which arise out of the earth. 18 But the saints of the Most High shall receive the kingdom, and possess the kingdom forever, even forever and ever.' 19 "Then I wished to know the truth about the fourth beast, which was different from all the others, exceedingly dreadful, with its teeth of iron and its nails of bronze, which devoured, broke in pieces, and trampled the residue with its feet; 20 and the ten horns that were on its head, and the other horn which came up, before which three fell, namely, that horn which had eyes and a mouth which spoke pompous words, whose appearance was greater than his fellows. 21 **"I was watching; and the same horn was making war against the saints, and prevailing against them, 22 until the Ancient of Days came, and a judgment was made in favor of the saints of the Most High, and the time came for the saints to possess the kingdom.**

Compare to:

Revelation 17:7-14 "But the angel said to me, "Why did you marvel? **I will tell you the mystery** of the woman and of **the beast** that carries her, which has the seven heads and the **ten horns**. The beast that you saw was, and is not, and will ascend out of the bottomless pit and go to perdition. And those who dwell on the earth will marvel, whose names are not written in the Book of Life from the foundation of the world, when they *see the beast that was, and is not, and yet is. "Here is the mind which has wisdom: The seven heads are seven mountains on which the woman sits. There are also seven kings. Five have fallen, one is, and the other has not yet come. And when he comes, he must continue for a short time. The beast that was, and is not, is himself also the eighth, and is of the seven, and is going to perdition. "The **ten horn**s which you saw are ten kings who have received no kingdom as yet, but they receive authority for one hour as kings with the beast. These are of one mind, and they will give their power and authority to the beast. These will make war with the Lamb, and the Lamb will overcome them, for He is Lord of lords and King of kings; and those who are with Him are called, chosen, and faithful."*

We could make a lot of speculations here, but the point of this book is making connections to the Old Testament. Do we see *The Language* matching up? Do we see *The Big Picture* consistently using the Beast(s) to represent the world system? And by making these connections, can we better understand some of the more confusing parts of the book of Revelation?

- Big Question: Is there more than one Beast in Revelation? We see the Harlot riding a Beast, and then we see 10 horns at war with the Harlot. Is that for 'control' of the Beast? Can the Beast be controlled? And what about the 'Man of Perdition' being also called 'The Beast'?

Chapter 25: The Harlot

Isaiah 23: 16-18, "Take a harp, go about the city, You forgotten **harlot;** *Make sweet melody, sing many songs, - That you may be remembered." And it shall be, at the end of seventy years, that the Lord will deal with Tyre. She will return to her hire,* **and commit fornication with all the kingdoms of the world on the face of the earth.** *Her gain and her pay will be set apart for the Lord; it will not be treasured nor laid up, for her gain will be for those who dwell before the LORD, to eat sufficiently, and for fine clothing."*

Compare to:

Revelation 17:1-2 "Come, I will show you the judgment of **the great harlot** *who sits on many waters,* **2 with whom the kings of the earth committed fornication,** *and the inhabitants of the earth were made drunk with the wine of her fornication."*

And:

*Isaiah 47:8-13 "Therefore hear this now, **you who are given to pleasures**, who dwell securely, who say in your heart, '**I am, and there is no one else besides me; I shall not sit as a widow,** nor shall I know the loss of children'; But these two things **shall come to you in a moment, in one day**: the loss of children, and widowhood. They shall come upon you in their fullness **because of the multitude of your sorceries**, for the great abundance of your enchantments. "For you have trusted in your wickedness;*
You have said, 'No one sees me';
*your wisdom and your knowledge have warped you; And you have said in your heart, '**I am, and there is no one else besides me.**'*
Therefore evil shall come upon you; you shall not know from where it arises.
And trouble shall fall upon you; you will not be able to put it off. And desolation shall come upon you suddenly, which you shall not know. "Stand now with your enchantments

and the multitude of your sorceries,"

<u>Compare to</u>:

*Revelation 18:4-24 "And I heard another voice from heaven saying, "Come out of her, my people, lest you share in her sins, and lest you receive of her plagues. For her sins have reached to heaven, and God has remembered her iniquities. Render to her just as she rendered to you, and repay her double according to her works; in the cup which she has mixed, mix double for her. In the measure that she glorified herself and **lived luxuriously**, in the same measure give her torment and sorrow; for she says in her heart, **'I sit as queen, and am no widow, and will not see sorrow**.' Therefore her **plagues will come in one day**—death and mourning and famine. And she will be utterly burned with fire, for strong is the Lord God who judges her. "The kings of the earth who committed fornication and lived luxuriously with her will weep and lament for her, when they see the smoke of her burning, standing at a distance for fear of her torment, saying, 'Alas, alas, that great city Babylon, that*

mighty city! **For in one hour your judgment has come.'** "And the merchants of the earth will weep and mourn over her, for no one buys their merchandise anymore: merchandise of gold and silver, precious stones and pearls, fine linen and purple, silk and scarlet, every kind of citron wood, every kind of object of ivory, every kind of object of most precious wood, bronze, iron, and marble; and cinnamon and incense, fragrant oil and frankincense, wine and oil, fine flour and wheat, cattle and sheep, horses and chariots, and bodies and souls of men. The fruit that your soul longed for has gone from you, and all the things which are rich and splendid have gone from you, and you shall find them no more at all. The merchants of these things, who became rich by her, will stand at a distance for fear of her torment, weeping and wailing, and saying, 'Alas, alas, that great city that was clothed in fine linen, purple, and scarlet, and adorned with gold and precious stones and pearls! **For in one hour such great riches came to nothing.'** Every shipmaster, all who travel by ship, sailors, and as many as trade on the sea, stood at a distance and cried out *when they saw the smoke of her burning, saying, 'What is like this great city?' "They threw dust on their heads and cried out, weeping and wailing, and saying, 'Alas, alas, that great city, in which all who had ships on the sea became rich by her wealth!* **For in one hour she is made desolate**.' *"Rejoice over her, O heaven, and you holy apostles and prophets, for God has avenged you on her!" Then a mighty angel took up a stone like a great millstone and threw it into the sea, saying, "Thus with violence the great city Babylon shall be thrown down, and shall not be found anymore. The sound of harpists, musicians, flutists, and trumpeters shall not be heard in you anymore. No craftsman of any craft shall be found in you anymore, and the sound of a millstone shall not be heard in you anymore. The light of a lamp shall not shine in you anymore, and the voice of bridegroom and bride shall not be heard in you anymore. For your merchants were the great men of the earth,* **for by your sorcery all the nations were deceived.** *And in her was found the blood of prophets and saints, and of all who were slain on the earth."*

<u>And compare to</u>:

*Nahum 3:4, "because of the multitude of harlotries of **the seductive harlot,** The mistress of **sorceries, Who sells nations through her harlotries,** And families through her **sorceries**."*

- Big Question: Is this harlot figure a demonic spirit who has warred against righteousness through time? Is this symbolic of a nation or people who sell sexual immorality to other nations? Is the United States in danger of being a nation who sells sexual immorality to the world, whether through Hollywood, online pornography, political policies?

Chapter 26: The Bowls

Revelation 15: 5-8 *"After these things I looked, and behold,* **the temple of the tabernacle of the testimony** *in heaven* **was opened.** *And* **out of the temple** *came the seven angels having the seven plagues,* **clothed in pure bright linen, and having their chests girded with golden bands.** *Then one of the four living creatures gave to the seven angels seven golden* **bowls** *full of the wrath of God who lives forever and ever.* **The temple** *was filled with smoke from the glory of God and from His power,* **and no one was able to enter the temple till the seven plagues of the seven angels were completed."**

Compare to:

Exodus 25:32-34, **"Three bowls** *shall be made like almond blossoms on one branch, with an ornamental knob and a flower, and three bowls made like almond* *blossoms on the other branch, with an ornamental knob and a flower— and so for the six branches that come out of the lampstand. On the lampstand itself **four bowls** shall be made like almond blossoms, each with its ornamental knob and flower."* (Seven bowls total for the construction of the Tabernacle of the Wilderness).

And

*2 Chronicles 4:6 "He also made **ten lavers (bowls)**, and put five on the right side and five on the left, to wash in them; such things as they offered for the burnt offering they would wash in them, but the Sea was for the priests to wash in. 7 And he made ten lampstands of gold according to their design, and set them in the temple, five on the right side and five on the left. 8 He also made ten tables, and placed them in the temple, five on the right side and five on the left. **And he made one hundred bowls** of gold. 9 Furthermore he made the court of the priests, and the great court and doors for the court; and he overlaid these doors with bronze. 10 He set* *the Sea on the right side, toward the southeast. 11 Then Huram made the pots and the shovels and the **bowls**.*

The Chiasm is a great tool when we look at the seven bowls and the seven plagues. The beginning of the Holy Bible starts with a showdown between a false god and the true God. The true God demonstrates His ultimate control over Earth, and He does this by pouring out ten plagues on Egypt. God glorifies His name through His demonstration of power and devastation. Now, in Revelation, the end of the Bible mirrors the beginning of the Bible. Another false god, the Antichrist, wars against the true God. And just like the Exodus story, in the last days, the true God, once again, will glorify His name through His demonstration of power and devastation on Earth when He pours out His wrath on the disobedient.

- Big Question: How closely do these bowls match plagues which God brought upon Egypt in the story of the exodus? Which plagues are missing?

Chapter 27: The Leviticus Calendar

Leviticus 23 Feasts

The Sabbaths		Jesus is the Lord of the Sabbath Matt.12:8, Mark 2:28, Luke 6:5
Passover and Unleavened Bread		Fulfilled on the Cross
First Fruits		Fulfilled at the Resurrection
Weeks or Pentecost		Fulfilled in Acts 2:1
Trumpets		unfulfilled
Day of Atonement		unfulfilled
Tabernacles		unfulfilled

The God of Creation put things into our daily lives as proof of Himself, like fingerprints of who He is. Have you ever asked yourself why do we, as people, go into a death-like coma called sleep every night and awaken to a new day? Why does going to sleep and waking up have similarities with the resurrection? Or, why do we as people have to eat something that dies so we can have life? Plants are living things. Cows and chickens are living things. Yet we find life in the sacrificial death of something else. Could it be that these mechanisms are given to us as proof of the gospel story and eternal life? *The Big Picture* of the gospel is hidden in plain sight all around us.

The following passage is from Leviticus 23. It's a list of the feasts that the Lord God wants His people to celebrate. As you go through the passage, use your tools. Ask what part of *The Big Picture* each feast connects with. Look at *The Language*. And now that you are aware of *The Chiasm* of scripture, try to see how these feasts might be relevant to the Book of Revelation.

> *"And the Lord spoke to Moses, saying, "Speak to the children of Israel, and say to them: 'The feasts of the Lord, which you shall proclaim to be holy convocations, these are My feasts." Leviticus 23:1.* **(The Sabbath)** *'Six days shall work be done, but the seventh day is a Sabbath of solemn rest, a holy convocation. You shall do no work on it; it is the Sabbath of the Lord in all your dwellings.* **(The Passover and Unleavened Bread)** *'These are the feasts of the Lord, holy convocations which you*

shall proclaim at their appointed times. On the fourteenth day of the first month at twilight is the Lord's Passover. And on the fifteenth day of the same month is the Feast of Unleavened Bread to the Lord; seven days you must eat unleavened bread. On the first day you shall have a holy convocation; you shall do no customary work on it. But you shall offer an offering made by fire to the Lord for seven days. The seventh day shall be a holy convocation; you shall do no customary work on it.' "

(The Feast of Firstfruits) *And the Lord spoke to Moses, saying, "Speak to the children of Israel, and say to them: 'When you come into the land which I give to you, and reap its harvest, then you shall bring a sheaf of the firstfruits of your harvest to the priest. He shall wave the sheaf before the Lord, to be accepted on your behalf; on the day after the Sabbath the priest shall wave it. And you shall offer on that day, when you wave the sheaf,* **a male lamb** *of the first year,* **without blemish,** *as* *a burnt offering to the Lord. Its grain offering shall be two-tenths of an ephah of fine flour mixed with oil, an offering made by fire to the Lord, for a sweet aroma; and its drink offering shall be of wine, one-fourth of a hin. You shall eat neither bread nor parched grain nor fresh grain until the same day that you have brought an offering to your God;* **it shall be a statute forever throughout your generations in all your dwellings.**

(The Feast of Weeks) *'And you shall count for yourselves from the day after the Sabbath, from the day that you brought the sheaf of the wave offering: seven Sabbaths shall be completed.* **Count fifty days** *to the day after the seventh Sabbath; then you shall offer a new grain offering to the Lord. You shall bring from your dwellings two wave loaves of two-tenths of an ephah. They shall be of fine flour; they shall be baked with leaven.* **They are the firstfruits to the Lord.** *And you shall offer with the bread seven lambs of the first year, without* blemish, one young bull, and two rams. They shall be as a burnt offering to the Lord, with their grain offering and their drink offerings, an offering made by fire for a sweet aroma to the Lord. Then you shall sacrifice one kid of the goats as a sin offering, and two male lambs of the first year as a sacrifice of a peace offering. The priest shall wave them with the bread of the firstfruits as a wave offering before the Lord, with the two lambs. They shall be holy to the Lord for the priest. And you shall proclaim on the same day that it is a holy convocation to you. You shall do no customary work on it. **It shall be a statute forever in all your dwellings throughout your generations**. 'When you reap the harvest of your land, you shall not wholly reap the corners of your field when you reap, nor shall you gather any gleaning from your harvest. You shall leave them for the poor and for the stranger: I am the Lord your God.'

(The Feast of Trumpets) Then the Lord spoke to Moses, saying, "Speak to the children of Israel, saying: 'In the seventh month, on the first day of the month, you shall have a sabbath-rest, **a memorial of blowing of trumpets**, a holy convocation. You shall do no customary work on it; and you shall offer an offering made by fire to the LORD.' "

(The Day of Atonement) And the LORD spoke to Moses, saying: "Also the tenth day of this seventh month shall be the Day of Atonement. It shall be a holy convocation for you; you shall afflict your souls, and offer an offering made by fire to the Lord. And you shall do no work on that same day, for it is the Day of Atonement, to make atonement for you before the Lord your God. **For any person who is not afflicted in soul on that same day shall be cut off from his people.** And any person who does any work on that same day, that person I will destroy from among his people. You shall do no manner of work; **it shall be a statute forever throughout your generations in all your dwellings**. It shall be to you a *sabbath of solemn rest, and you shall afflict your souls; on the ninth day of the month at evening, from evening to evening, you shall celebrate your sabbath."*

(The Feast of Tabernacles)*Then the Lord spoke to Moses, saying, "Speak to the children of Israel, saying: 'The fifteenth day of this seventh month shall be the Feast of Tabernacles for seven days to the Lord. On the first day there shall be a holy convocation. You shall do no customary work on it. For seven days you shall offer an offering made by fire to the Lord. On the eighth day you shall have a holy convocation, and you shall offer an offering made by fire to the Lord. It is a sacred assembly, and you shall do no customary work on it. **'These are the feasts of the Lord which you shall proclaim to be holy convocations**, to offer an offering made by fire to the Lord, a burnt offering and a grain offering, a sacrifice and drink offerings, everything on its day— besides the Sabbaths of the Lord, besides your* gifts, besides all your vows, and besides all your freewill offerings which you give to the Lord. 'Also on the fifteenth day of the seventh month, when you have gathered in the fruit of the land, you shall keep the feast of the LORD for seven days; on the first day there shall be a sabbath-rest, and on the eighth day a sabbath-rest. And you shall take for yourselves on the first day the fruit of beautiful trees, branches of palm trees, the boughs of leafy trees, and willows of the brook; and you shall rejoice before the Lord your God for seven days. You shall keep it as a feast to the Lord for seven days in the year. **It shall be a statute forever in your generations.** You shall celebrate it in the seventh month. You shall dwell in booths for seven days. All who are native Israelites shall dwell in booths, that your generations may know that I made the children of Israel dwell in booths when I brought them out of the land of Egypt: I am the Lord your God.' " So Moses declared to the

*children of Israel the feasts of the
Lord.*

Did you make any connections from this passage to the future Revelation? Did you see a Calendar here? We have seven feasts like we have seven days in a week. Is that relevant? Let's think this through and ask some questions. Why do we have 365 days in a year? Because that is the time the Earth takes to revolve around the Sun. Why do we have roughly 28 days per month? Because that's the time it takes the moon to revolve around the Earth, depending on your views of the calendar. But why do we have seven days in a week? Think about it for a minute. There is no reason scientifically to divide time into seven days. So why do we do it? And why is the week accepted everywhere on this planet? Well, you can thank Jesus for a seven day week. Because outside of the creation story in Genesis, there is no reason for a seven day week.

Going back to Chapter 23 in Leviticus, let's look a little closer at this calendar. And let's use *The Language* in reverse, Let's view this Old Testament passage through our understanding of Jesus and the New Testament. Do we see the fulfillment of the events **in Jesus**?

The Sabbath: Jesus said He was the *'Lord of the Sabbath'*? Did you notice from the opening verse above, Lord God chooses to celebrate the Sabbath?

> *Leviticus 23:1, "And the Lord spoke to Moses, saying, "Speak to the children of Israel, and say to them: 'The feasts of the Lord, which you shall proclaim to be holy convocations, **these are My feasts**."*

This is the first event of our calendar of feasts. We can see this as the first day of the week, which some of the churches now celebrate as Sunday, and it's because He rose again on the first day of the week. We see the fulfillment of the Sabbath **in Jesus's** redemption and restoration, which is by His victory on the cross and His resurrection from the dead.

The Passover and Unleavened Bread: It was on the night of the Passover that Jesus was betrayed. Did you know from the beginning, Matzah bread is required to be striped and pierced? Why? Because Jesus is the *"Bread of Life"*, and in fulfillment of the unleavened bread's requirement, Jesus was striped and pierced. And

Jesus is *"The Lamb of God who takes away the sin of the World"* (John 1:36), so **in Jesus**, we see the feast of the Passover and Unleavened Bread fulfilled.

The Feast of Firstfruits: Can we think of any New Testament Language tying Jesus to this feast?

*1 Corinthians 15: 20-23, **"But now Christ has risen from the dead, and has become the firstfruits** of those who have fallen asleep. For since by man came death, by Man also came the resurrection of the dead. For as in Adam all die, even so in Christ all shall be made alive. But each one in his own order: **Christ the firstfruits**, afterward those who are Christ's at His coming."*

Because the Apostle Paul sees Jesus as the *'first fruits'*, I think it's safe for us to agree. **In Jesus** we see the feast of First Fruits fulfilled.

The Feast of Weeks: Now this might not sound as familiar to modern Christians, but look through the description for anything that stands out. Does fifty days sound familiar? It was 50 days after the resurrection, in Acts chapter 1, we see the Holy Spirit poured out on the church. This is the day of Pentecost. *Pentekoste* is the number

50 in Greek. This is not coincidental. Those 50 days were destined before time began. The Author and Finisher of our faith makes Himself known through the fulfillment of the prophecies in His Word.

> *Isaiah 46: 9-11, "For I am God, and there is no other; I am God, and there is none like Me, **Declaring the end from the beginning; And from ancient times things that are not yet done**, saying, 'My counsel shall stand, And I will do all My pleasure,'"*

And so it was **in Jesus**, by the pouring out of His Holy Spirit on the Church, on the Day of Pentecost, that we see the fulfillment of the Feast of Weeks. (Galatians 4:6)

The Feast of Trumpets: Do we see Jesus in this feast? And do we see this feast fulfilled **in Jesus**? The answer here is: 'No, **not yet**'.

> *Matthew 24: 29-31,* **"Immediately after the tribulation of those days** *the sun will be darkened, and the moon will not give its light; the stars will fall from heaven, and the powers of the*

*heavens will be shaken. Then the sign of the Son of Man will appear in heaven, and then all the tribes of the earth will mourn, **and they will see the Son of Man coming on the clouds of heaven with power and great glory**. And He will send His angels **with a great sound of a trumpet**, and they will gather together His elect from the four winds, from one end of heaven to the other."*

The Feast of Trumpets has not yet been fulfilled **in Jesus.** Up to this point on our calendar, we have seen the fulfillment of each of these feasts in Jesus. But from this event on, according to the way we've reviewed the first four feasts, we won't see them fulfilled, yet, in Jesus. And the keyword is *yet*.

The Day of Atonement: In my opinion, the Day of Atonement *is* The Book of Revelation. If you're looking for a lens with which to see The Book of Revelation through, try seeing the whole Book of Revelation as the Day of Atonement. I believe all the events, all the scenes, all the Language of Revelation directly correlates to the Day of Atonement in Heaven. This is one of my favorite connections to John's Revelation.

Perhaps the next book I will write will be: The Book of Revelation is the final Day of Atonement. But as for seeing the fulfillment of the Day of Atonement in Jesus, again, we can say 'not yet'.

The Feast of the Tabernacles: As with the last two feasts, we are still waiting for this feast to be fulfilled **in Jesus**. If we see the end mirroring the beginning, through *The Chiasm*, could we ask some questions here? Could the bride of Jesus have a temporary time of dwelling 'in booths' after the resurrection but before the 1000 year reign? Could this be part of Jesus's promise to "prepare a place for us" in Heaven, although we also are promised to rule Earth with Him?

- Big Question: Would you consider using this Leviticus Calendar in evangelism? Can we trust God's plan from the beginning to the end? Does this encourage you in Jesus? And is it shocking, despite all of Satan's attempts to thwart the promises of God, Satan can't stop even one promise? Did you know there are over 8,000 promises in the Holy Bible, and not one of them has, or can be, stopped by Satan? Who is Like Our Great God and Saviour?

Chapter 28: 1260 Days

Revelation 11:3 *'And I will give power to my two witnesses, and they will prophesy* **one thousand two hundred and sixty days**, *clothed in sackcloth."*

And on the opposite side of the chiastic structure:

Revelation 12:5 & 6 " She bore a male Child who was to rule all nations with a rod of iron. And her Child was caught up to God and His throne. Then the woman fled into the wilderness, where she had a place prepared by God, that they should feed her there **one thousand two hundred and sixty days**."

This has got to be one of the strongest proofs I can find for *our Chiasm*. And it's also proof for our *Apex* of Revelation 11:15.

Just as we saw in the Noah chiasm, there should be matching letters or numbers on both sides of The Apex. That's exactly what we see here in *The Chiasm* of Revelation. If you go a couple verses forwards or back from The Apex in Revelation 11:15-19 you will find "**1260 days**".

Again, this is massively important if you want to let Scripture interpret Scripture. Let's watch Scripture interpret Scripture here in a very simple way. We are going to take something confusing and allow *The Chiasm* to give us the interpretation. Are you ready for this?

> *Revelation 12:14 "But the woman was given two wings of a great eagle, that she might fly into the wilderness to her place, where she is nourished **for a time and times and half a time**, from the presence of the serpent."*

What does that mean? What amount of time is 'for a time and times and half a time'? Pay attention, what you are about to learn gives you the answer from Scripture itself. This is not about you trusting someone else's interpretation. This is you seeing for yourself the answer in Scripture, for your own eyes.

We know *the Apex* of the Chiasm is in chapter 11:1. And we find this confusing term as we read forwards in the lower section. So, for the answer, let's go backwards in the passage, to the upper section and look for the explanation. We are looking for a period of time **before** *the Apex*, (but not the 1260– that already has a match). Can you see a period of time in Revelation chapter 11:3?

Look below, and see the Chiasm like a math equation. We can plug in the matching sections, with *the Apex* in the middle.

C) "forty two months" (Rev. 11:3)
B)   1260 Days (Rev. 11:3)
APEX   Jesus is King (Rev. 11:15-19)
B)   1260 Days (Rev. 12:6)
C) **"a time and times and half a time"**
       (Rev. 12:14)

Answer: *Revelation 11:2 "And they will tread the holy city underfoot for **forty-two months**."*

Do you see it? We have **two time references;** "1260 days'- which matches before and after *the Apex*. And we have 'forty two months'. But because we *already* have a match in the chiastic structure for the '1260 days' on both sides of The Apex, then the next two time frames are a match; **'a time and times and a half a time'** **equals** **'forty two months'. The chiasm provides the answer.** This is scripture interpreting scripture! We just have to use our tools.

- Big Question: What other connections can you find using *The Chiasm?* Why are these chapters so cryptic?

Chapter 29: The Battle of Armageddon

Ezekiel 38:18 "And it will come to pass at the same time, when Gog comes against the land of Israel," says the Lord GOD, *"that My fury will show in My face. 19 For in My jealousy and in the fire of My wrath I have spoken: 'Surely in that day there shall be* **a great earthquake** *in the land of Israel, 20 so that the fish of the sea, the birds of the heavens, the beasts of the field, all creeping things that creep on the earth,* **and all men who are on the face of the earth shall shake** *at My presence. The mountains shall be thrown down, the steep places shall fall, and every wall shall fall to the ground.' 21 I will call for a sword against Gog throughout all My mountains,"* says the Lord GOD. *"Every man's sword will be against his brother. 22 And I will bring him to judgment with pestilence and bloodshed; I will rain down on him, on his troops, and on the many peoples who are with him, flooding rain,* **great hailstones,** *fire, and brimstone. 23 Thus I will magnify Myself and sanctify Myself, and I will be known* **in the eyes of many**

nations. *Then they shall know that I am the LORD."'*

<u>Compare to</u>:

>*Revelation 16:16 And they gathered them together to the place called in Hebrew,* **Armageddon**. *17 Then the seventh angel poured out his bowl into the air, and a loud voice came out of the temple of heaven, from the throne, saying, "It is done!" 18 And there were noises and thunderings and lightnings; and there was* **a great earthquake, such a mighty and great earthquake as had not occurred since men were on the earth**. *19 Now the great city was divided into three parts, and the cities of the nations fell. And great Babylon was remembered before God, to give her the cup of the wine of the fierceness of His wrath. 20 Then every island fled away, and the mountains were not found. 21* **And great hail** *from heaven fell upon men, each* **hailstone** *about the weight of a talent.* **Men blasphemed God** *because of the plague of* **the hail**, *since that plague was exceedingly great."*

When comparing passages like this, I think it becomes overwhelmingly obvious that these are the same events with witnesses in both the Old and New Testaments. What do you think?

- Big Question: Do the Old Testament passages seem to hold more or less detail? Can we add missing pieces of detail from the Old Testaments for a clearer picture?

Chapter 30: The Feast of the Lord

For starters, please do not confuse this feast with the Wedding Feast of the Lamb. Yes, there are **two feasts** in Revelation 19. So let's go ahead and separate these two feasts. *Chapter 34: Return of the King* will cover the Marriage Feast of the Lamb, for the church, while this chapter will cover the Feast of the Lord, which is for the wicked.

And by now, because you are familiar with the chiastic structure, you would be expecting two feasts, on either side of Christ's return, right? (Chapter 34 will have an illustration of that.)

If we keep the Old Testament in mind as we go through Revelation, we can add all the elements together to better see *the Big Picture*.

In Revelation chapter nineteen, **The Feast of the Lord** is briefly mentioned, but not by name, following the Lord's return.

> *Revelation 19:17-18, "Then I saw an angel standing in the sun; and he cried with a loud voice,* **saying to all the birds that fly in the midst of heaven, "Come and gather together for the supper of the great God, that**

you may eat the flesh of kings, the flesh of captains, the flesh of mighty men, the flesh of horses and of those who sit on them, and the flesh of all people, free and slave, both small and great."

Compare to:

Ezekiel 39:*17 "And as for you, son of man, thus says the Lord God,* **'Speak to every sort of bird and to every beast of the field:** *"Assemble yourselves and come;* **gather together from all sides to My sacrificial meal** *which I am sacrificing for you, a* **great sacrificial meal on the mountains of Israel, that you may eat flesh and drink blood. 18 You shall eat the flesh of the mighty, drink the blood of the princes of the earth, of** *rams and lambs, of goats and bulls, all of them are fatlings of Bashan. 19 You shall eat fat till you are full, and drink blood till you are drunk, at My sacrificial meal which I am* *sacrificing for you. 20 **You shall be filled at My table with horses and riders, with mighty men and with all the men of war,"** says the Lord GOD."*

This has yet to be fulfilled. In context, this portion of Ezekiel is all about the coming 'Day of the Lord'. We can get several connections from Ezekiel to the Book of Revelation. But if we are simply reading Revelation on its own, we might miss some great connections to even more details from the Old Testament, and those connections are easily made by *The Language*.

Next, let's connect the Feast of The Lord from Ezekiel to a misunderstanding the Disciples had. See if you spot the connection:

Luke 17: 34-37, "I tell you, in that night there will be two men in one bed: the one will be taken and the other will be left. Two women will be grinding together: the one will be taken and the other left. Two men will be in the field: the one will be taken and the other left." And they answered and said to Him, "Where, Lord?" So He said to them, **"Wherever the body is, there** *the eagles will be gathered together."*

Where is Jesus saying these people are taken? He's reminding the Disciples of Ezekiel's prophecy of the Feast of the Lord. I know I might lose some of you here, so look back at the passages for yourself. Can you see there are two gatherings? **Two gatherings**.

In Matthew 24, Jesus says "And He will send His angels with a great sound of a trumpet, and they will gather together His elect from the four winds, from one end of heaven to the other." That's *one* gathering. Then, and this is important to get, –<u>before there were chapter breaks</u>, Jesus continued speaking... into Matthew 25 saying,

> *Matthew 25:31-33,* **"When the Son of Man comes in His glory, and all the holy angels with Him,** *then He will sit on the throne of His glory.* **All the nations will be gathered before Him,** *and He will separate them one from another, as a shepherd divides his sheep from the goats. And He will set the sheep on His right hand, but the goats on the left."*

What do you see here? A gathering of *everyone*. The saints are gathered first, then the lost are gathered, and everyone is being separated into groups. Why?

I Corinthians 6:9, ***"Do you not know that the unrighteous <u>will not inherit</u> the kingdom of God?"***

The unsaved, the lost, the rebellious CANNOT inherit the Kingdom of Jesus Christ. Plain and simple. And we will rule and reign with Him on Earth. This is not just a heavenly kingdom, but an earthly kingdom as well. Then, the Will of God will be done "on Earth as it is in Heaven". Anyone with the Mark of The Beast will be killed. Anyone who has declared their rebellion against Jesus Christ, and pledged allegiance to Satan by receiving the Mark of the Beast, has to die.

Luke 19:25 "But bring here those enemies of mine, who did not want me to reign over them, and slay them before me.' "

In Revelation 19, we see Jesus, coming in all His Glory, with the angels of Heaven -- so this matches up with what Jesus said in Matthew 25. And in that same passage, Jesus tells us the saints will be gathered to meet Him in the air, and the wicked will be gathered for destruction. This slaughter of the rebellious is also prophesied in Zephaniah.

> *Zephaniah 1:7 & 8 "Be silent in the presence of the Lord God; For the day of the Lord is at hand,* **For the Lord has prepared a sacrifice; He has invited His guests**. *"And it shall be, In the day of the Lord's sacrifice, That I will punish the princes and the king's children, And all such as are clothed with foreign apparel. In the same day I will punish All those who leap over the threshold, Who fill their masters' houses with violence and deceit."*

Look at the prophecy below, from Revelation. Can you see two harvests, or two gatherings?

> *Revelation 14:14 "Then I looked, and behold, a white cloud, and on the cloud sat <u>One like the Son of Man</u>, having on His head a golden crown, and in His hand a sharp sickle. 15 And another angel came*

*out of the temple, crying with a loud voice to Him who sat on the cloud, "**Thrust in Your sickle and reap**, for the time has come for You to reap, **for the harvest of the earth is ripe**." 16 So He who sat on the cloud thrust in His sickle on the earth, and the earth was reaped. 17 <u>Then another angel came out of the temple which is in heaven, he also having a sharp sickle.</u> 18 And another angel came out from the altar, who had power over fire, and he cried with a loud cry to him who had the sharp sickle, saying, "**Thrust in your sharp sickle and gather the clusters of the vine of the earth, for her grapes are fully ripe**." 19 So the angel thrust his sickle into the earth and gathered the vine of the earth, and threw it into the great winepress of the wrath of God. 20 And the winepress was trampled outside the city, and blood came out of the winepress, up to the horses' bridles, for one thousand six hundred furlongs."*

- Big Question: Does studying Revelation motivate you to evangelize? If we truly believe this is the future of mankind, should this motivate us to share the good news of Jesus as much as we can? How could you use your knowledge of the last days in spreading the gospel of Jesus?

Chapter 31: The War on the Saints

Daniel clearly records, by saying it repeatedly, that in the last days there will be a war on the saints. The Beast will be given authority over the saints, and the saints will be killed. This war on the saints is also mentioned several times in Revelation.

Daniel 7: 21-22, "I was watching; and the same horn **was making war against the saints, and prevailing against them**, until the Ancient of Days came, and a judgment was made in favor of the saints of the Most High, and the time came for the saints to possess the kingdom."

Daniel 8:24, "His power shall be mighty, but not by his own power; He shall destroy fearfully, And shall prosper and thrive; **He shall destroy the mighty, and also the holy people.**"

Compare to:

Revelation 6:10-11, "And they cried with a loud voice, saying, "How long, O Lord, holy and true, until You judge and avenge our blood on those who dwell on the earth?" Then a white robe was given to each of them; and it was said to them that they should rest a little while longer, **until both the number of their fellow servants and their brethren, who would be killed as they were, was completed."**

Revelation 7:14, "these are the ones (killed) who come out of the great tribulation".

Rev 12:17, "And the dragon was enraged with the woman, and he went to **make war with the rest of her offspring,** *who keep the commandments of God and have the testimony of Jesus Christ."*

Rev 13:7, "It was granted to him **to make war with the saints and to overcome them.** *And* *authority was given him over every tribe, tongue, and nation."*

Revelation 14: 12-13, "Here is the patience of the saints; here are those who keep the commandments of God and the faith of Jesus. Then I heard a voice from heaven saying to me, "Write: **'Blessed are the dead who die in the Lord from now on.'** *" "Yes," says the Spirit, "that they may rest from their labors, and their works follow them."*

In the Old Testament, through the prophet Isaiah, God warns His people for the upcoming war on the saints.

Isaiah 26: 20-21, **"Come, my people, enter your chambers, And shut your doors behind you; Hide yourself, as it were, for a little moment, Until the indignation is past.** *For behold, the LORD comes out of His place To punish the inhabitants of the earth for their iniquity; The earth will also disclose her blood, And will no more cover her slain.*

- Big Question: What does a war on the saints look like? Is it a spiritual war on the peace, patience, contentment of the saints? Or do you think it's a war in the physical world? How can and does Satan defeat the saints?

Chapter 32: The Great Earthquake with Hail

Revelation 16:17, *"Then the seventh angel poured out his bowl into the air, and a loud voice came out of the temple of heaven, from the throne, saying, "It is done!"* 18 *And there were noises and thunderings and lightnings; and there was* **a great earthquake, such a mighty and great earthquake as had not occurred since men were on the earth.** 19 *Now the great city was divided into three parts, and the cities of the nations fell. And great Babylon was remembered before God, to give her the cup of the wine of the fierceness of His wrath.* 20 *Then every island fled away, and the mountains were not found.* 21 **And great hail from heaven fell upon men, each hailstone about the weight of a talent.** *Men blasphemed God because of the plague of hail, since that plague was exceedingly great."*

Compare to:

Ezekiel 38:19- 23, **"Surely in that day there shall be a great** *earthquake in the land of Israel, 20 so that the fish of the sea, the birds of the heavens, the beasts of the field, all creeping things that creep on the earth, **and all men who are on the face of the earth shall shake at My presence.** The mountains shall be thrown down, the steep places shall fall, and every wall shall fall to the ground.' 21 I will call for a sword against Gog throughout all My mountains," says the Lord GOD. "Every man's sword will be against his brother. 22 And I will bring him to judgment with pestilence and bloodshed; I will rain down on him, on his troops, and on the many peoples who are with him, flooding rain, **great hailstones**, fire, and brimstone. 23 Thus I will magnify Myself and sanctify Myself, and I will be known in the eyes of many nations. Then they shall know that I am the LORD."*

- Big Question: How can the world survive such a devastating event? If you put all the plagues, death, and destruction together, what would the earth look like at the end of Revelation? Would earth, without plants and trees, and rivers of blood, look like another planet?

Chapter 33: The Earth Harvested

Joel 3:12, "Let the nations be awakened, and come up to the Valley of Jehoshaphat; For there I will sit to judge all the surrounding nations. 13 **Put in the sickle, for the harvest is ripe.** *Come, go down; For the winepress is full, The vats overflow— For their wickedness is great." 14 Multitudes, multitudes in the valley of decision! For the day of the LORD is near in the valley of decision.*

<u>Compare to</u>:

Revelation 14:14, "Then I looked, and behold, a white cloud, and on the cloud sat One like the Son of Man, having on His head a golden crown, and in His hand a sharp sickle. 15 And another angel came out of the temple, crying with a loud voice to Him who sat on the cloud, **"Thrust in Your sickle and reap,** *for the time has come for You to reap,* **for the harvest of the earth is ripe."** *16 So He who sat on the cloud thrust in His sickle on the earth, and the earth was reaped. 17 Then another*

angel came out of the temple which is in heaven, he also having a sharp sickle. 18 And another angel came out from the altar, who had power over fire, and he cried with a loud cry to him who had the sharp sickle, saying, "Thrust in your sharp sickle and gather the clusters of the vine of the earth, for her grapes are fully ripe." 19 So the angel thrust his sickle into the earth and gathered the vine of the earth, and threw it into the great winepress of the wrath of God. 20 And the winepress was trampled outside the city, and blood came out of the winepress, up to the horses' bridles, for one thousand six hundred furlongs."

- Big Question: Why is 'the harvest' mentioned here, in chapter 14 of Revelation? And the return of the King in chapter 19? Is this truly sequential? Or without time consideration?

Chapter 34: The Return of the King

Today, in modern day Israel, the Mount of Olives is a gigantic cemetery. Take a moment, and search online, "Mount of Olives cemetery". What do you see? And do you know why? The answer lies in the Old Testament.

> *Zechariah 14: 3, "Then the LORD will go forth and fight against those nations, as He fights on the day of battle. 4. **And in that day His feet will stand on the Mount of Olives**," .*

The Jewish people know this prophecy, and are both waiting and planning on it to be fulfilled on the day of the Lord. By being buried on the Mount of Olives, a person can guarantee, they will be one of the first to resurrect on the Day of the Lord. Therefore, owning a plot in Mount of Olives is extremely valuable.

But this information is not found in the New Testament. What other details of the Lord's return could we find in the Old Testament? Well, to start with, did you know by both Testaments, tell us it is Jesus who leads the army of the Lord?

Joshua 5:13, "And it came to pass, when Joshua was by Jericho, that he lifted his eyes and looked, and behold, a Man stood opposite him with His sword drawn in His hand. And Joshua went to Him and said to Him, "Are You for us or for our adversaries?" 14 So He said, **"No, but as Commander of the army of the Lord I have now come.***" And Joshua fell on his face to the earth and worshiped, and said to Him, "What does my Lord say to His servant?" 15 Then the Commander of the Lord's army said to Joshua,* **"Take your sandal off your foot, for the place where you stand is holy.***" And Joshua did so."*

Consider what Man can make the ground He walks on holy. And what Man is worthy to lead the Armies of the Lord? This question is answered when we see Jesus Christ, the Son of Man, leading the Army of the Lord upon His return.

Revelation 19:11, "Now I saw heaven opened, and behold, a white horse. And He who sat on him was called Faithful and True, and in righteousness He judges and makes war. 12 His eyes were like a flame of fire, and on His head were many crowns. He had a name written that no one knew except Himself. 13 He was clothed with a robe dipped in blood, and His name is called The Word of God. 14 **And the armies in heaven, clothed in fine linen, white and clean, followed Him on white horses**. *15 Now out of His mouth goes a sharp sword, that with it He should strike the nations. And He Himself will rule them with a rod of iron. He Himself treads the winepress of the fierceness and wrath of Almighty God. 16 And He has on His robe and on His thigh a name written:*

'KING OF KINGS AND LORD OF LORDS'."

This is at Armageddon. It's neat to look at *the Language* of the prophet Joel, and how he records this location and what happens in this valley.

Joel 3:12-14 **"Let the nations be awakened**, *and come up to the Valley of Jehoshaphat;* **For there I will sit to** *judge all the surrounding nations"* ... *"Multitudes, multitudes in the valley of decision! For the day of the LORD is near in the valley of decision.".*

It's interesting that Joel saw this place as the valley of decision. People have to make a choice, of life in Jesus, or death for eternity.

The Day of the Lord is everywhere in the Old Testament. In fact, there are so many more details available to us in the Old Testament, which can really paint some vivid scenes when imagining the return of Jesus Christ.

Zechariah 14: 12-15 "And this shall be the plague with which the LORD will strike all the people who fought against Jerusalem: Their flesh shall dissolve while they stand on their feet, Their eyes shall dissolve in their sockets, And their tongues shall dissolve in their mouths. It shall come to pass on that day that a great panic from the LORD will be among them. Everyone will seize the hand of his neighbor, And raise his hand against his neighbor's hand; Judah also will fight at Jerusalem. And the wealth of

*all the surrounding nations shall be
gathered together: Gold, silver, and
apparel in great abundance. Such
also shall be the plague.On the horse
and the mule, On the camel and the
donkey, And on all the cattle that
will be in those camps.So shall this
plague be."*

Before we move into the next chapter, I
want to add this here. Within the larger chiasm of
Revelation, there are several smaller chiasms.
Some span several chapters, others just a couple
verses. Below is a smaller chiasm hidden within
Revelation 19. I found this myself. I was curious
about when the 'marriage feast of the lamb'
would be. By reading this chapter over and over
and looking for patterns, I took time in meditation
and prayer to the Lord Jesus. After a day or so,
He gave this to me:

B) *Revelation 19:7, "Let us be glad
and rejoice and give Him glory, for
the marriage of the Lamb has come,
and His wife has made herself
ready." 8 And to her it was granted
to be arrayed in fine linen, clean and
bright, for the fine linen is the
righteous acts of the saints. 9 Then*

*he said to me, "Write: '**Blessed are those who are called** to the **marriage supper of the Lamb!' "***
(This is a feast declared and the saints gathered for the feast)

> **(APEX)** *Revelation 19:11, "Now I saw heaven opened, and behold, a white horse. And He who sat on him was called Faithful and True, and in righteousness He judges and makes war. 12 His eyes were like a flame of fire, and on His head were many crowns. He had a name written that no one knew except Himself. 13 He was clothed with a robe dipped in blood, and His name is called The Word of God. 14 And the armies in heaven, clothed in fine linen, white and clean, followed Him on white horses. 15 Now out of His mouth goes a sharp sword, that with it He should strike the nations. And He Himself will rule them with a rod of iron. He Himself treads the*

*winepress of the fierceness
and wrath of Almighty God.
16 And He has on His robe and
on His thigh a name written:
'KING OF KINGS AND LORD
OF LORDS'."*

B) *Revelation 19:17 "...saying to all
the birds that fly in the midst of
heaven, "**Come and gather
together for the supper of the
great God**, 18 that you may eat the
flesh of kings, the flesh of captains,
the flesh of mighty men, the flesh of
horses and of those who sit on them,
and the flesh of all people, free and
slave, both small and great." 19 And
I saw **the beast, the kings of the
earth, and their armies,
gathered together** to make war
against Him who sat on the horse
and against His army."*
**(This is a feast declared and the
damned gathered for the feast)**

- Big Question: What other fascinating details
  can you find about the return of Jesus Christ?
  What does the Old Testament say about
  Jesus's Second Coming?

Chapter 35: The River and Tree of Life

*Revelation 22:2-5, "And he showed me a pure **river of water of life,** clear as crystal, **proceeding from the throne of God and of the Lamb.** In the middle of its street, and on either side of the river, was **the tree of life**, which bore twelve fruits, each tree yielding its fruit every month. **The leaves of the tree were for the healing of the nations.** And there shall be no more curse, but the throne of God and of the Lamb shall be in it, and His servants shall serve Him. They shall see His face, and His name shall be on their foreheads. There shall be no night there: They need no lamp nor light of the sun, for the Lord God gives them light. And they shall reign forever and ever."*

Compare to:

Ezekiel 47:1-12, "Then he brought me back to the door of the temple; and **there was water, flowing from under the threshold of the temple** toward the east, for the front of the temple faced east; **the water was flowing** from under the right side of the temple, south of the altar. He brought me out by way of the north gate, and led me around on the outside to the outer gateway that faces east; and **there was water,** running out on the right side. And when the man went out to the east with the line in his hand, he measured one thousand cubits, and he brought me through the waters; **the water** came up to my ankles. Again he measured one thousand and brought me through **the waters**; the water came up to my knees. Again he measured one thousand and brought me through; the water came up to my waist. Again he measured one thousand, and it was a river that I could not cross; for the water was too deep, water in which one must swim, a river that could not be crossed. He said to me, "Son of man, have you seen this?" Then he brought me and returned me **to the bank of the river.** When I returned, there, along *the bank of the river, were very many trees on one side and the other. Then he said to me: "This water flows toward the eastern region, goes down into the valley, and enters the sea. When it reaches the sea, its waters are healed.* **And it shall be that every living thing that moves, wherever the rivers go, will live.** *There will be a very great multitude of fish,* **because these waters go there; for they will be healed, and everything will live wherever the river goes.** *It shall be that fishermen will stand by it from En Gedi to En Eglaim; they will be places for spreading their nets. Their fish will be of the same kinds as the fish of the Great Sea, exceedingly many. But its swamps and marshes will not be healed; they will be given over to salt. Along the bank of the river, on this side and that, will grow all kinds of trees used for food; their leaves will not wither, and their fruit will not fail. They will bear fruit every month, because their water flows from the sanctuary. Their fruit will be for food,* **and their leaves for medicine."**

- Big Question: Why does the Bible open and close in a garden? What is the significance of a River of Life? What do you think about the Tree of Life producing twelve different fruits? Did you interpret this as twelve trees, or one tree that changes fruit each month? Which fruits do you think will come from The Tree of Life?

Chapter 36: The Two Resurrections

*Revelation 20:5-6, "But the rest of the dead did not live again until the thousand years were finished. This is the **first** resurrection. Blessed and holy is he who has part in the **first** resurrection."*

There are **two** resurrections.

Daniel 12:1-4, "At that time Michael shall stand up, The great prince who stands watch over the sons of your people; And there shall be a time of trouble, such as never was since there was a nation, even to that time. And at that time your people shall be delivered, everyone who is found written in the book. ***And many of those who sleep in the dust of the earth shall awake, some to everlasting life, some to shame and everlasting]contempt.*** *Those who are wise shall shine like the brightness of the firmament, and those who turn many to righteousness. Like the* *stars forever and ever. "But you, Daniel, shut up the words, and seal the book until the time of the end; many shall run to and fro, and knowledge shall increase."*

<u>Compare to</u>:

*Revelation 20:4-15, "And I saw thrones, and they sat on them, and judgment was committed to them. Then I saw the souls of those who had been beheaded for their witness to Jesus and for the word of God, who had not worshiped the beast or his image, and had not received his mark on their foreheads or on their hands. And they lived and reigned with Christ for a thousand years. But the rest of the dead did not live again until the thousand years were finished. **This is the first resurrection. Blessed and holy is he who has part in the first resurrection**. Over such the second death has no power, but they shall be priests of God and of Christ, and shall reign with Him a thousand years. Now when the*

*thousand years have expired, Satan will be released from his prison and will go out to deceive the nations which are in the four corners of the earth, Gog and Magog, to gather them together to battle, whose number is as the sand of the sea. They went up on the breadth of the earth and surrounded the camp of the saints and the beloved city. And fire came down from God out of heaven and devoured them. The devil, who deceived them, was cast into the lake of fire and brimstone where the beast and the false prophet are. And they will be tormented day and night forever and ever. Then I saw a great white throne and Him who sat on it, from whose face the earth and the heaven fled away. And there was found no place for them. **And I saw the dead, small and great, standing before God, and books were opened.** And another book was opened, which is the Book of Life. And the dead were judged according to their works, by the things which were written in the books. **The sea*** *gave up the dead who were in it, and Death and Hades delivered up the dead who were in them.* And they were judged, each one according to his works. Then Death and Hades were cast into the lake of fire. This is the second death. *And anyone not found written in the Book of Life was cast into the lake of fire.*"

- Big Question: Where else do we find resurrection in the Old Testament? What does Job 19: 25-26 say? Do you believe the resurrection of 'Dry Bones' in Ezekiel 37 was real or metaphorical?

Chapter 37: Three People Groups

*Zechariah 14:16, "And it shall come to pass that **everyone who is left of all the nations** which came against Jerusalem shall go up from year to year to worship the King, the Lord of hosts, and to keep the Feast of Tabernacles."*

Have you ever asked yourself, when we rule with Jesus in His Kingdom, who do we rule over? I mean the Holy Bible is clear that we do sit on the throne with Jesus, and we do rule and reign with Him as kings and priests forever. But **who** do we rule over?

At this point, pull out your Bible, if you don't already have it next to you, and turn to Zechariah chapter 12. Take five minutes to read from chapter 12 til the end of the book.

C) Jerusalem Delivered. (Zech.12:1-9)

B)   The Messiah. (Zech. 12:10)

Apex) False Worship Destroyed (Zech.13:2-6)

B)   The Messiah. (Zech. 13:7-9)

C) Jerusalem Renewed. (Zech. 14:16-21)

What are you seeing? We are close to the end of this book. Have you learned to see *The Big Picture* and apply it to the text? Are you seeing

The Language, and connecting it with parts of Revelation? Did you catch *The Chiasm* in Zechariah?

The tools work if you work them. Back to the original question, who are we reigning over in the Kingdom of Jesus Christ? Well, it looks like there might be three groups. In Revelation, we know that God's people are marked on their foreheads, let's call that group one. And we know that Satan copy-cats this with the mark of the beast, so well call Satan's people group two.

> *Zechariah 14:16, "And it shall come to pass that **everyone who is left of all the nations which came against Jerusalem** shall go up from year to year to worship the King, the LORD of hosts, and to keep the Feast of Tabernacles."*

This group from above cannot be saints because we are gathered to Him upon His return, to rule and reign with Him-- that's group one. But these can't have the mark of the beast on them, because all of Satan's followers are slain at the Feast of the Lord, (chapter 30: Feast of the Lord), that's group two. I'm going to suggest it might be everyone who is left, **that did not choose a side**. It might be a very small group, but there seems to be people who didn't accept the mark of the beast but also didn't receive Jesus as their Lord.

Maybe there is a group of people living in the Himalayas that missed all the action. Or maybe one of the small islands never got involved with the mayhem of the last days. Who knows? But the passage above tells us 'that whoever is left', continues living. This would be group three.

The existence of group three might explain a few things. The Bible tells us Jesus will *'rule with a rod of iron'* (Rev. 19:15). If only saints remained, why would this be necessary? But if there is a world repopulated by non-saints, this would make sense.

This would also explain the Ezekiel temple, and the sacrifices we see in it. If God is indeed present with mankind, and these people still have freewill and choice, then there would be a need for atonement... which at this point could not be Jesus. **The atonement by Jesus was by faith**, for those who believed in Him. Now that Jesus sits on the earthly throne, there is a need for faith. The vicarious atonement by faith is no longer an option. The surviving mankind would need atonement via sacrifices.

This would also explain Isaiah's prophecies of the millennial reign:

> *Isaiah 65: 20, "No more shall an infant from there live but a few days, nor an old man who has not fulfilled his days;* ***For the child shall die one hundred years old, but the sinner being one***

hundred years old shall be accursed.* 21 *"They shall build houses and inhabit them; They shall plant vineyards and eat their fruit.* 22 *"They shall not build and another inhabit; They shall not plant and another eat;* **For as the days of a tree, so shall be the days of My people***, and My elect shall long enjoy the work of their hands.* 23 *"They shall not labor in vain, nor bring forth children for trouble;*
For they shall be the descendants of the blessed of the Lord, **and their offspring with them***. 24 *"It shall come to pass that before they call, I will answer;*
And while they are still speaking, I will hear. 25 *"The wolf and the lamb shall feed together, the lion shall eat straw like the ox, and dust shall be the serpent's food. They shall not hurt nor destroy in all My holy mountain," says the Lord."*

If only saints remained, then how would a child die, even at a hundred years, and how would there be a sinner (65:20)? If we remember *the Big Picture* and *the Chiasm*, the restoration of Jesus brings mankind back to the beginning. It looks like the end of mankind will mirror the days of Adam.

And this third group of people would also explain the last rebellion. In Revelation chapter 20, the Holy Bible tells us Satan is locked away for 1000 years, after which he is released. He then leads mankind in one last rebellion. Which should make us ask with whom? Well, maybe this third people group has not made their choice. For 1000 years, they will watch the Earth flourish under the rule of Jesus Christ and His saints, but they will still have to make a choice. Satan will most likely use the same lie as in the beginning: "you could be our own gods". And a third of mankind will rebel. Again, the rebellion makes sense if the third people group never made a choice prior to the return of Jesus. Who else would rebel? The saints? Not likely.

And finally, this third people group, and their choice to serve Jesus or rebel, might explain why after this the Earth is burned up, and the Lord Jesus creates a new Heaven and a new Earth. It would be a new beginning, and a new world where all mankind has personally made the choice to worship Jesus.

- Big Question: Do you think the existence of a third people group lines up with the Book of Revelation? What other prophecies from the Bible would make sense with a third people group? If you disagree with a third people group, who else might we reign over?

Chapter 38: In Closing

Isaiah 42:8-9, "I am the LORD, that is My name; And My glory I will not give to another, ...Behold, the former things have come to pass, and new things I declare; Before they spring forth, I will tell you of them."

In closing, let's recap what we've accomplished together. We took the time to diligently search the Old Testament for a better understanding of the book of Revelation. This brings to mind one of my favorite verses,

*Matthew 13:52, "Then Jesus said to them, **"Therefore every scribe instructed concerning the kingdom of heaven is like a householder who brings out of his treasure things new and old."***

We've done just that. We've dug into the most precious gift on Earth, the Holy Bible, and we've brought out 'things new and old'. There is nothing more incredible on our planet than the

Word of God, given to us, passed down with integrity, and held together by the infinitely powerful will of God Our Father. The Holy Bible is truly a treasure to behold. It's packed full of promises for those who need promises in tough times. It's charged with hope for those in need of light during dark days. It's brimming with wisdom for anyone in need of direction. It's the beacon of Truth for those bombarded with deception. And in it is life, by and through and to Jesus Christ.

> *Romans 11:33 "Oh, the depth of the riches both of the wisdom and knowledge of God! How unsearchable are His judgments and His ways past finding out! 34 "For who has known the mind of the LORD? Or who has become His counselor?" 35 "Or who has first given to Him and it shall be repaid to him?" 36* **For of Him and through Him and to Him are all things, to whom be glory forever. Amen"**

We've learned to step back sometimes and reevaluate a text in light of **The Big Picture.** We stepped back from just seeing The Book of Revelation alone. We took the time to include the basic gospel of Restoration and Redemption as we studied together. We saw the end of the Holy Bible bring us back to the beginning, back into a paradise garden and back into a holy relationship with our Creator.

We've learned to watch **The Language** of the texts. The wording was purposely used by the Author to be connections to the past. We learned those connections are a wonderful guide for interpretation. Now we can look forward and back, having more context, more details, and more understanding.

We learned **The Chiasm**. What an interesting tool the Hebrew writers left us. We learned to let Scripture emphasize the main point of a text. We saw the chiasm give us a way to split the book of Revelation in half, allowing one side to better interpret the other side.

And we took the second half of this book to compare some of the most essential, key elements of Revelation to the Old Testament. We used our tools to analyze, connect and ask questions, because we've learned that the book of Revelation is not a stand-alone testimony of the 'end of days'.

In closing, let me share with you some of my hopes. I hope, because of this book, we all become better students of the Holy Bible. I hope each of us, knowing what the future holds, become evangelists who are on fire for Jesus. I sincerely hope that we become strong defenders of our faith because of our study time in His Word. But more than all of these, I hope we all grow In Jesus. I hope that our time spent together, digging through, wrestling with, and making His Word a part of who we are, -'*eating the scroll*'- **that we fall more in love with Jesus**, Amen.

2 Peter 3:17, "You therefore, beloved,... beware lest you also fall from your own steadfastness, being led away with the error of the wicked; 18 **but grow in the grace and knowledge of our Lord and Savior Jesus Christ. To Him be the glory both now and forever. Amen.***"*

*If you enjoyed this book, and through it, you saw Jesus highly exalted, please take 2 minutes to leave a Good Review on Amazon Kindle.

If you support the Great Commission, consider sponsoring us as your missionaries as we serve full time in Guatemala City. You can learn more about Jackie and me on our website, MessengersforJesus.com

A Very Special Thankyou To Pastor Matthew Butterfield and Venture Church of Easley, South Carolina.

Made in the USA
Columbia, SC
02 September 2024

41416699R10124